The best way to predict your future is to create it. —Abraham Lincoln.

DESIGN

YOUR

DESTINY

Actualizing Your Birthright To Success

THE
CORNERSTONE
PUBLISHING

HENRY A. UKAZU

DESIGN YOUR DESTINY
Actualizing Your Birthright To Success

Copyright © 2017 by **Henry A. Ukazu**

ISBN-13: 978-1543237535
ISBN-10: 1543237533

Published By:
Cornerstone Publishing
A division of Cornerstone Creativity Group LLC
+1 516-547-4999 | Info@thecornerstonepublishers.com
www.thecornerstonepublishers.com

Author's Information
For speaking engagement or to order books
by Henry Ukazu Call +1 (646)-399-4443 or
email: Henrous@gmail.com

For Publishing Consultation,
Please email: Raregempublishers@gmail.com

DEDICATION

To my mother, **Lolo Agnes Ukazu;** and my grandmother, **Mrs. Roseline Ukazu.**

To my late father, **Chief Anthony Lazarus Merenwanne (Ajeje) Ukazu** - a man who sacrificed his life and all he had to bequeath to me a life of true purpose and authentic meaning. He loved education with a passion, which made him to weather all odds to give his children quality education.

Special recognition goes to my immediate family **Chief & Dr (Mrs) Moses Ukazu, Mr. Anthony Ukazu, Mrs Lilian Ibejiuba, Mr & Mrs George Ukazu and Ms. Cynthia Oluchi Ukazu.** And also to my all my cousins, uncles and aunts.

To everyone who couldn't discover themselves before exiting this world; and to those who are yet to discover themselves.

ACKNOWLEDGMENTS

Pre-eminently, I give special gratitude to God, who alone made me what I am today. I am particularly grateful for the strength, knowledge, wisdom, understanding and insight accorded me by His grace, to write this book under the guidance of the Holy Spirit.

I thank my family for their continual support all through the period of solitude I had to endure to write this book. I also thank my 'second mother', Ms. Chetachi Ecton, CEO, When In Need Foundation, the woman who God used to inspire me to write this book in just eight weeks!

Profound gratitude goes to two of my life mentors, Dr. Yomi Garnett, who painstakingly edited this work and produced the masterpiece you now hold in your hands; and Dr. Dele Momodu - former presidential candidate in Nigeria and founder of Ovation International Magazine and Ovation Television - who continues to patiently inspire and motivate me.

I am indebted to Dr. Olumide Abayomi, who literally took me by the hands to mentor me. He was there for me whenever I reached out to him for advice, despite his work itineraries between the United States and Nigeria. I also thank Ola Aboderin, who assisted in editing this book.

I sincerely thank Dr. Uchenna Ekwo for his fatherly support during the most critical and defining moments of my life, and for believing in me despite my obvious lapses. I thank Ms. Georgina Galanis for guiding me in the art of meditation as a daily practice.

A word of gratitude to Mr. Rotimi Oni (DHS Hero Director), the man who stabilized my professional career in the United States of America, and Dr. Kinglsey Nwokedi, for his outstanding support during my trying times in the United States.

I also appreciate Chika Ibejiuba, founder and president of Wonder Boy Entertainment, for his gracious assistance and mentorship. I thank Rev. Fr. Steven Masinde, Rev. Fr. Augustine Odinakalu, Rev. Fr. Ocul Charles and Rev. Fr. Casmir Onyegwara for their prayers.

It's worthy to mention some of my bosom friends who supported me during this journey. Ms. Nwaneka Okoyejim, Calistus Uwakwe Esq., Paschal Nwakuna Esq., Mr. Rock Ndukwe, Valerie J. Frade, Prof. Chidi Odinakalu, Ms. Nkemdilim Okafor Esq, Mrs. Anne Mmeje Esq, Mr. Joseph Onyebuchi, Mrs. Kate Amadi, Mr. Allen Hope, Mr. Chimbuo Dominic Esq, Dr. Linda Iheme, Mr. Ezeh Umeh Oleka Esq, Mr. Obioma Ajawuihe, Mrs. Roseline Umeh Esq, Mr. Franklin Osuchukwu, and Mr. Dozie David.

I cannot fail to mention and appreciate the great friends who believed in me, and assisted and contributed in one way or the other towards my growth and development. They include: Mpule Kwelagobe(Miss Universe 1999), Mr. Adegoke Tolulope, Mr. Madu Modestus Esq, Mr. Raphael Ibekwe, Dr. Obinna Obi, Emeka Obi, Ms. Matthews Aisha, Professor Gail Lewis and Nnaemeka Ndukwe, Dr. George Ohakamnu, Dr. Nogzi Ochei, Mr. Uzoma Dire, Mr. Nmandi Dire, Dr. Chiamaka Diala, Ms. Peace Okoye,

Mrs. Uju Anyakoha, Ms.Gloria Emerigbo, Mr. Ugonna Onuoha, Mr. Christian Nwanedo, Mr. Anthony Chima, Mr. Dominic Ifidon, Mr. Gbenga Omotayo, Ms. Ezinne Adaugo Jane Nwokocha, Dr. Sylvester Okere, Pastor Isidore A. Agoha, Ms. Lilian Egbuchulem, Professor Gregory Nkemjika, Ms. Anyikwa Chimdindu MaryRose, Pastor Gbenga Showunmi, Ms. Mary Olushoga, Mr. Ferdinand Ubozoh Esq., Lucy Kanu, Mr. Aaron Carr, Assembly man Michael Blake, Ms. Simone- Monet Wahls, Ms. Nwadiaro Obianuju, Mr. Chinaemerem Muoka, Mr. Modest Ibe, Mr. Tonye Rex Idaminabo Esq., Mrs. Florence Onyegue Esq., Ms. Nepken Osuan, Mr. Faith Abiodun, Mr. Joseph Awadjie, Ms. Ogechi Agim, Mr. Dapo Ibrahim, Mr. Nsonya Chidi, Dr. Queen Ememe, Mr. Ugochukwu Dike, Hon. Barr. C.M.C, former Minority Leader in Imo State House of Assembly in Nigeria, Mr. Onwuchekwa Uche Kelvin, Ogwo Nwankwo, Mr. Nmandi Mbata, Mr. Uma Ota, Chinwe Obinwa, Dr. Nicoline Ambe, Mr. Moses Siloko Siasa, Mr. Okenfe Lebarty, Dr. Augustine Okereke, Nkechi Ogbodo, founder, Kechie's Project Inc, Dr. Nkechi Agwu, Ms. Astrid Sylvester, Professor Ken Nwogu, Rev. Fr. Emmauel Edeh, founder, Madonna University, Jamie Pajoel, Mr. Emmanuel Magege, Dr. Nkechi Agwu, Mr. Jerry Ottih, Mr. Emmanuel Ohuabunwa, Mr. Emmanuel Ebizie, Mr. Friday Onuche, Mr. Chima Sixtus Irejiogu, Mr. Austin Ogbodo, Jude Onah, Okpara Gerald Ugochukwu, Mr. Kingsley Nkurum, Mr. Chibuike Nwoke, Mr. Chinonye Ugoeze, Mr. Eva Nwoke, Mr. Alex Agu, Ms. Anuli Faustina Ibeh, Mr. Ibeh Cyril Chinedu, Mr. Simon Utsu, Mr. Kelechi Osuchukwu, Ms. Ogechi Oparah, Dr. Shade Bernard, Francisca Anieke, Mr. Nigel Hamilton and Mr. Emmanuel Obidigbo. Mr. Beroro Efekoro, Mr. Ugochukwu Egboluche, Mr. Chinonso Anozie Esq, Ms. Marilyn Oma Anoma, HRH Eze Chima Dimoriaku (Ezeamara), Ms. Augustina Enechile Abraham.

I deeply appreciate the staff of Freeman Houses, who have

continued to epitomize the value of family and friends - and thus creating an atmosphere of understanding and teamwork. These include Ms. Maritza Alvarez (Executive Director, Seneca Houses); Ms. Grace Arvelo (Director, Freeman Houses); Ms. Felisia Williams (Supervisor), Mrs. Elbia Cabral, Linda Ebinum, and Ms. Wanda Perez.

I would like to express a special word of gratitude to my indefatigable uncle and tax mentor, Chief Chuba Ohams (Onwa Imo), who has never failed to show me love and support whenever I reach out to him for assistance. I am particularly grateful for his gracious assistance all through the process of writing and publishing this book.

I am grateful to the staffs and members of Mary-Ola Nursery and Primary School; Federal Government College, Okigwe; Madonna University, Okija; Nigerian Law School, Abuja; and the National Youth Service Corps (Nigeria) for contributing to my life success.

I absolutely cannot fail to mention the staff and students of New York Law School for their kind assistance and the opportunity given to me to prove myself during my graduate program. Special thanks to Prof. Ann Thomas (Dean, Graduate Tax Program), Mrs. Sharon Brown, Oral Hope (Registrar), Anthony Crowell (Dean. New York Law School), Professor Diane L. Fahey, Vicky Ocasio and Katrice Ayarza.

A special gratitude goes to the United States of America which provided me with the enabling opportunities to unleash the potentials and opportunities in me. Truly, America is a land of opportunities which will spur you to succeed if you work hard and play by the rules. Without the enabling infrastructural facilities, it would have been difficult for me to accomplish this feat. May God continue to bless America.

I must acknowledge the role of some of the influential people in the Nigerian Lawyers Association who assisted me with opportunities during my formative years in the United States of America. These are Mr. Shamsey Oloko Esq, Partner at Thorgood Law Firm; Mr. Oliver Mbamara Esq, Administrative Law Judge; Mr. Billy Enobakhare Esq; Ms. Nnenna Onua Esq; Mrs. Shereefat Balogun Esq; Mrs. Nkasi Okafor Esq; Mr. Unekuojo Idachaba Esq; Mr. Nexus Sea Esq; Stella Azie Esq; Mr. Chijioke Metu Esq; Mr. Placid Agunwa Esq; Mr. Uche Elemadu Esq; Mr. John Edozie Esq; Mr. John Emefieh Esq; and Ms. Folake Ayoola Esq.

FOREWORD

I feel profoundly honored to be invited to write the foreword to this illuminating piece of literary effort. This, for me, is an opportunity to express a sincere word of goodwill and commendation on the brilliant excursion into the world of motivation and inspiration that the author has elected to embark upon.

As an author myself, it is not only a source of the most profound pleasure but also one of immense professional gratification for me to have the privilege of endorsing the work of an exceptional person. That is why I feel uncommonly fortunate to have the rare privilege of, not only celebrating the work of the Henry Ukazu a valued protégé of mine, but also being the recipient of the honor of commenting on his written work.

I have no doubt whatsoever that in writing this book, the author has been motivated by a genuine desire to create a handbook of functional utility that would consist of positive and uplifting thoughts that will inspire anyone in need of guidance. In my educated opinion, this is a book of simple truths from many different philosophies and disciplines that will serve that purpose.

Most people seemingly live in a poignant state of constant despair and silent desperation. This, for the most part, is because most people tragically lack coping mechanisms for the constant challenges

11

that come their way in their bid to actualize themselves in a world in constant and distressing flux. Additionally, most people simply do not possess a clue as to how to launch themselves on the process of self-discovery, which is so paramount to setting them on the path to the authentic success they so fervently crave. The writer aims, with this book, *"Design Your Destiny,"* to imbue in the reader, a renewed hope, by offering inspiring thoughts and messages. Its carefully-thought-out quotes and premium nuggets of wisdom are educational, uplifting, emotive, and life-transforming, in the ultimate hope that the entire package will serve as a tool for both coping with the stress of day to day living, and launching every reader on the road to genuine transformational awareness.

Success and happiness are almost always dependent on certain kinds of thoughts that habitually traverse our minds. Therefore, it becomes highly imperative that we condition our minds to the right kind of mental activity. In my opinion, this is the beauty that is inherent in this comprehensively inspirational book, in which the author has synthesized a compendium of brilliant facts and thoughts that will set almost anyone on the path to genuine success.

Indeed, this book is a gift from the body, mind, and soul of the author to you, the reader.

It is my prayer that you will, like me, draw out tremendous inspiration from the pages of this book, such that you will have renewed hope in a life that you can live with more confidence and faith.

DELE MOMODU
CEO and Publisher of Ovation International

CONTENTS

PREFACE

This book was written under divine guidance. I urge you to read it with rapt and meditative attention. Refuse to read it as you would read a novel, or the commonplace inspirational or empowerment book. It should be approached as a work of enlightenment, whose purpose is to unravel the hidden, inner qualities of a soul in search of self-discovery, and on the path to genuine success in life.

Within this volume are nuggets that will help you to discover who you truly are, what you were created for, the true meaning and purpose of life, and, of course, how you will ultimately succeed in life. Moreover, since much of the book focuses on human productivity, it will enlighten you and open your mind to make you think out of the box. It will educate and inspire you. It will inform, reform and transform you. Above all, it will make you see the change which you desire in your life. It will do all these because its aim is to make you succeed.

You certainly need this book if you are on the path of self-discovery and are committed to a never-ending search for authentic wisdom. It has been structured, in compliance with contemporary trends, for easy assimilation. Composed of ten chapters, the layout is such that allows for easy flow of thought and comprehension.

I strongly recommend that you read this book with the rapt concentration you would accord any material of an academic nature; it is composed of truly concentrated facts, presented mostly in a condensed manner.

According to Albert Einstein, the most complicated thing in the world is tax. We will assume that he said this because he couldn't comprehend what tax is all about. I shared the same feeling with Einstein, while studying Taxation Law at New York Law School in a graduate program. However, with a strong determination to learn, I was able to demystify tax as I gained experience in the field.

Albert Einstein was globally acknowledged to be a genius. Ironically, he was the same man who would provide one of my favorite quotes of all time: "Everybody is a genius, but if you judge a fish by its ability to climb a tree, it will forever think it is stupid." He was right in this assertion.

As human beings, we are all unique and created for different purposes, in addition to being endowed with varying degrees of understanding. The irony here is that Albert Einstein, despite being a genius, still found a universally practiced subject such as taxation so complex. He, however, hit the nail on the head with the above quote. That, indeed, is the irony and beauty of life. It is upon this premise that this book is built.

As you proceed on your life journey, questions that will arise in your mind include: "What is the meaning of life?" "What is its purpose?" Once you start asking yourself questions like these, it means that you have begun your own journey to self-discovery, and answers will be on their way. The truth is, unless you understand the essence of these ingrained questions, you would have a hard time finding the answers. This is because you cannot find the answers in books. At best, they would set you on the path to self-discovery, while you would have to live through them to witness your own transformation.

According to Barry Manilow, "I believe that we are who we choose to be. Nobody is going to come and save you. You've got to save yourself. Nobody is going to give you anything. You've got to go out and fight for it. Nobody knows what you want, except you; and nobody will be as sorry as you if you don't get it. So don't give up your dreams."

I agree with this saying because nobody knows you more than you know yourself. This book will also assist you in unraveling some of the potentials inherent in you by challenging you to become uncommonly creative and resourceful, in addition to shaping you to succeed in life.

Experience has shown that the most difficult thing in the world is understanding oneself. Indeed, understanding yourself is the biggest hurdle you can ever overcome in the journey of designing your destiny. As the popular saying goes, "life is all about understanding."

Two friends might have a mutual issue to resolve. However, how they approach the issue is what will determine how big, or how trivial the issue really is. Put differently, it is their mutual understanding that will lead to a perfect resolution of the problem. Is it not true that when we identify a problem, it is already fifty percent solved? Is it not also true that you cannot solve any problem unless you have a good understanding of the issue?

For a lawyer to effectively represent a client, he or she needs to know the applicable laws in a particular court, as well as corresponding nuances, exceptions, and complex interpretations.

For example, a criminal lawyer would not be best suited in housing court. Doctors require tests to diagnose the ailments of their patients. The list is endless. Human beings can be quite difficult to understand, and this is because it can be very difficult to control or manage their emotions, being very unpredictable beings.

Man has a fundamentally inquisitive nature. I believe that this sublime, inquisitive nature of man finds basis in the Creator's declaration that, "Let us make man in our own image" (Genesis 1:26). The essence is for man to be exceptional in every way. After creating man, God gave him dominion over all creatures - to name them, in addition to controlling them. It is my belief that the combination of man's inability to understand himself perfectly, and his inquisitive nature, eventually led to his downfall in the Garden. We can reasonably assume that if Adam and Eve had known their strengths and weaknesses, they would have been able to establish their limits, and not eaten the forbidden fruit.

Ultimately, coming into an understanding of oneself is no mean achievement. It takes considerable time and deep introspection to arrive at this understanding and actualizing your birthright to success. It is a journey which, once embarked upon with deep commitment, can only lead to a sense of fulfillment, especially as it will make meaning of the mystery called life.

Finally, it should be noted that this is not an exhaustive way of discovering yourself or designing your destiny. Rather, see it as an insight to unravel some traits in you, which will enable you to further understand yourself and succeed in life.

HENRY A. UKAZU
New York, United States of America.

1

YOU WERE CREATED FOR A UNIQUE PURPOSE

Until you have figured out your life's purpose and the goal you are aiming for, you will only be existing and not living. —Anonymous

Has it ever occurred to you that you are not just like any other person on earth? If yes, have you ever wondered why this is so? Or to put the question in a different way, have you ever paused to ponder why you had to be born at a certain time, in a certain place and with certain traits that are unique to you?

The simple answer is: There is a unique mission for you to accomplish; a special vacuum for you to fill in the divine mandate given to humanity to explore and dominate the earth. You have a distinct role that you have been methodically fashioned to play in demonstrating the boundless possibilities of the gift of life that God has given to you.

Let's face it. Even human inventors and designers do not go to such elaborate lengths to create anything without having a definite purpose in mind for their creations. Why then would God, who is the embodiment of wisdom and strategy, devote time to designing a person, with features and attributes that are distinctly theirs, without a definite reason?

Just before the creation of the first man on earth, God indeed proved that the decision was a conscious and calculated one. He said, "Let Us make man in Our image, according to Our likeness; let them have dominion over the fish of the sea, over the birds of the air, and over the cattle, over all the earth and over every creeping thing that creeps on the earth" (Genesis 1:26).

What this really signifies is that every human on earth has a divinely-ordained mandate to fulfill. Therefore, given this responsibility and privilege, it becomes imperative for each one of us to engage in deliberate self-analysis and prayerful introspection to ascertain our purpose and assignment on earth.

According to Lao Tzu, "Knowing others is wisdom, knowing yourself is enlightenment." Understanding and knowing oneself is very important for living a purposeful, productive and fulfilled life. If you understand how your personality works, in addition to understanding yourself, you won't be moved by what other people think or say about you.

However, being yourself fully does not just happen. It takes great work and purposeful commitment. But the effort is worth it because, in knowing yourself, your life will be easier, and you will be able to confidently tackle any challenge that comes your way. The problem with most people is that they don't take time to understand themselves and their unique gifts.

DOWNSIDE OF SELF-DECEPTION

The worst thing that can happen to any person is lying to himself or herself. Telling lies to oneself is the greatest undoing to self. You can never lie to yourself and expect to be successful in life. So, you must know who you really are and gladly embrace your uniqueness and assignment. Once you understand yourself, it will be easy to adjust to any new development that may come your way.

Here is an illustration. Supposing you are preparing for an examination and you are wondering the best study method to use. Your ability to know when your mind is most productive and receptive to information will be a plus for you.

Regarding study methods, there are some people who prefer to study during quiet moments, like the early hours of the day, or at midnight when most people are sleeping. Some, on the other hand, may like to study with music, regardless of what time of the day it is. Over time, you would have discovered the best reading mode that aids better assimilation for you. The application of this knowledge of yourself is a demonstration of wisdom.

One major benefit of the journey of self-discovery or the process of gaining a better understanding of who you are is that it allows you to easily identify those life options that work for you and those that do not. This considerably reduces complications, frustrations and regrets on your journey.

TRACING YOUR ROOTS

According to Pablo Picasso, "The meaning of life is to find your gift and the purpose is to give it away." But the truth is that you can never know the meaning of life without knowing yourself and you can never know yourself without knowing the giver of life.

So, the foundation of knowing yourself is to know the creator of both yourself and your life.

To solve a problem, it's very important to fully understand the issues involved. Without understanding the issues, you can never get to the root cause of the problem, and neither will you be able to solve the problem. This is because identification of a problem means it is fifty percent solved. An African proverb says "if a person does not know where he's coming from, he won't know where he's going." This is true for any practical problem we want to solve.

For example, if you are given a mathematical problem to solve, and you don't know the right formula to use, it will be difficult to solve the problem. In law, if you have a legal case, and you don't know the issues involved, it will be difficult to litigate your case judiciously on behalf of your client; in medicine, a doctor relies on tests to diagnose an ailment, to give proper prescription and treatment.

The best way to get to the bottom of a situation is not to jump to conclusions, but to ask relevant questions. Most people don't really know themselves, either because they fail to search their inner self for the self-discovery of their strengths and weaknesses, or they fail to reach out to their creator.

The major reason most people fail in life is because they don't really discover themselves. Self-discovery is a life-long career because you can never fully comprehend yourself. You learn something about yourself daily. That is why you sometimes wonder how you were able to achieve a certain great feat or overcome a certain challenge. Everyday offers you a new opportunity to learn something new about yourself. In the words of Thomas Edison, "if we did everything we are capable of doing we would literally astound ourselves."

STICKING TO YOUR CALLING

Interestingly, there are some people who already know their calling in life but find it hard to keep to it. They prefer rather to do what pleases others, at the expense of living a focused and fulfilled life. Let me remind you that before you were born, God purposely fashioned you for a purpose; so do not ever think you came into the world by accident or that you need to please anyone to find fulfillment in life

God knew you before you were conceived in your mother's womb. He declares in Jeremiah 1:5, "Before I formed you in the womb I knew you; Before you were born I sanctified you; I ordained you a prophet to the nations." And then in Jeremiah 29:11, He says, "For I know the thoughts that I think toward you, thoughts of peace and not of evil, to give you a future and a hope."

Isn't this interesting? Before you were conceived, more than five hundred sperm cells were struggling to be you, but God chose you. That's sufficient to let you know you are not an accident. You might have had "illegitimate" parents because their bonding wasn't planned; but you are never an illegitimate child. God deliberately allowed your conception and eventual delivery. He could have easily prevented any of these; but He did not – because there is a great purpose for your life. You have a mission to fulfill in the world that no one else can!

STRIVING FOR SELF-MASTERY

I mentioned earlier that no human being can say with all certainty that he has fully discovered himself, because we are always evolving and learning new things about ourselves. A friend of mine, Marilyn Oma Anona, an inspirational blogger, once said,

"The three most difficult things in the world are steel, diamond and human beings."

You may differ on this, but I personally think she has a point especially as it relates to human beings. I say this because human beings are indeed the most wonderfully complex creatures you can ever imagine. Add the dynamism of their imaginations to the diversity of their physiological compositions and you might get a glimpse of what I am referring to here. No wonder the psalmist in Psalm 139:14 declares, "I will praise You, for I am fearfully and wonderfully made…"

As you consider the endless possibilities of the human mind, you would easily agree with me that conquering oneself is, indeed, the hallmark of success. Conquering yourself entails subduing the excesses of your instincts and temperament, and maximizing your various potentials till you are able to actualize your ultimate purpose on earth. I believe this was why Lao Tzu said, "He who has conquered the world is great. But he who has conquered himself is greater still."

So, how do you attain self-mastery? The journey of a thousand miles begins with a step in the right direction. Self-mastery begins with looking inwards and reflecting on your real strengths and weaknesses. Here is what you should know. If, for example, you are contesting for a particular position and everybody around you is telling you that can't succeed, what you should do is to listen to what your heart is telling you. If the whole world is telling you that you can't do it and you know you can do it, go ahead and do it - you will definitely succeed. Conversely, if the whole world is telling you that you can do it but you don't think you can, you are likely going to fail. The Scripture says in 1 John 4:4, "…He who is in you is greater than he who is in the world." Once you are able to realize who you are, the right opportunities will always come to you.

Success is a journey and not a destination, because it is not all about taking the first spot in any endeavor but maintaining it. The same ideology is applicable to life. As success-minded soldiers in the battle of life, we have to constantly devise survival strategies with which we can harness life's demands and vicissitudes to our advantage. The journey of life is a journey of faith, not a journey of approximations. It's a journey that requires conscious planning and resolve, as opposed to mere wishing and daydreaming, if you really want to succeed.

Nobody gets anything worthy in life without working towards it. It is a basic reality of life that opportunities only favor prepared minds. If you don't plan and work towards self-actualization, by stepping out of your comfort zone, you won't be able to achieve your dream. That is why Benjamin Franklin said, "Failing to prepare is preparing to fail."

If you don't ask, you won't get; if you don't seek, you won't find, and if you don't knock, the door won't be opened. If you don't go out, you will remain where you are. Therefore, you must seek the meaning of life by reaching out to the creator of heaven and earth to unravel the mysteries of your life, and seek a deeper understanding of yourself. Once you understand yourself, self-mastery becomes a piece of cake for you.

MAKING EXCELLENCE YOUR WATCHWORD

Nothing guarantees success and prosperity in life more than being known for excellence. Prosperity doesn't guarantee excellence, but excellence guarantees prosperity. Once you are good at what you do, humanity will definitely seek your services, not only because you are solving problems, but because you are adding value to lives and making the world a better place to live in.

The wise man in Proverbs 22:29 says it categorically, "Do you see a man who excels in his work? He will stand before kings; He will not stand before unknown men." That is an incontrovertible principle of success right there. If you don't have money, the reason is often because you are not solving a problem, or you are not solving enough problems, or you are not solving the right problem or you are not solving problems for the right people. Generally, we make money because we have something unique to offer to the world. It is simply a matter of fact that the world is in dire need of visionary leaders.

A major way to distinguish yourself from your contemporaries is to have a unique product or brand in the market. Once you are a unique brand, in addition to truly knowing yourself, you will never lack money.

BEING ORIGINAL

One of my favorite authors and mentors, John Mason, in his book, "Imitation is Limitation," emphasizes the importance of being original. God has endowed every one of us with certain qualities that make us unique. It's quite unfortunate, though, that many people die without living their true purpose. Dele Momodu, an international journalist and publisher, when asked the secret of his success, said: "Be yourself, work hard, have faith in God and believe in yourself."

You can never overestimate the importance of being original. When you are your true self, only true people will come to you; but when you compromise your identity and personality, only fake friends will come to you. So, strive always to be the best version of yourself, because it's only when you are honest and real to yourself that you will be able to truly actualize your potential in life. Be yourself. Tell yourself the truth, which only you know. In life, you can lie to others, but you can never lie to yourself.

The beauty of being original is that there's something which only you can do perfectly well, and with ease. You don't need to acquire much training, skill or even education to achieve this feat. This can be discovered by looking at what makes you happy. This aspect of life varies significantly; what works for Mr. A might not work for Mr. B. For example, someone may be very good at singing, while another is good at teaching, sports, leadership, entertainment, law, medical practice, journalism or electrical applications, and the list continues.

Most times, however, individuals, due to family, peer or societal pressure, venture into careers that are not suited to their calling, nature, and personality. Hence, they find it hard to succeed in such ventures or professions. Of course, such persons will never be happy while doing such unfitting work. Yet, in the journey of life, it's hard to succeed without being happy in what one is doing.

ROAD TO SELF-DISCOVERY

Self-discovery has become relatively easier in this era of social media. Many people have really come to discover who they are just by observing what they do for fun.

Personally, I discovered my true personality when I was in the university, though I had an idea during my high school days. Over time, I had seen myself speaking like an inspirational speaker, empowering and counseling people, adding value to the lives I came across and helping humanity in any little way I could. This passion led me to blogging, which saw me writing passionately about principles that make life meaningful and fulfilling.

It was within this period that a wonderful woman, Ms. Chetachi Ecton, the CEO of When In Need (WIN) Foundation—a 501(c)(3) organization that empowers the less-privileged in the society - gave me the prompting that I desperately needed to do something I had been lingering to do. She had adopted me as a protégé, and one day, she read one of my blog entries, titled, "The Little Things of Life". She said to me, "Have you considered writing a book?" It was only then that I gave writing a book some deep thought. In the past, I had thought about writing a book, but I kept procrastinating. Besides, I wasn't fully convinced I had what it takes to write. However, as soon as I became fully convinced I had what it takes to write, I keyed into the project.

I have come to discover that, in life, given every equal opportunity, everybody is a potential achiever; and we don't have dull brains, but only brains that are underdeveloped.

What I'm trying to point out here is that there are certain things that are so unique to you, if only you would look into yourself. Just don't allow anyone to belittle you or even define you. Say to yourself always, "Yes, I can do it."

I have said it earlier that nobody can know you more than you know yourself. Some people get to know themselves early in life; for others, it takes a much longer time. So, beloved, don't be hard on yourself. Just take it easy. And more importantly, develop a thriving relationship with God, who alone predetermined your coming into the world and fashioned you to fulfill your unique destiny.

The story is told about a man whose Ford car broke down while on a journey. This man knew a lot about cars and specifically this car, so he went to work. He tried different things and each time he went back to try and crank the engine, it still wouldn't start. A few minutes later, a large limousine pulled up beside him. Out stepped an old man who just stood and watched him for a few minutes.

Finally, the old man looked at him and told him to adjust a specific part on the engine. The young man was initially skeptical as it seemed unreasonable to him that the part mentioned by the old man could have caused the vehicle to break down. But then, after considering that he had tried every other thing he knew without succeeding, he thought he might as well give the old man's advice a shot. So, he adjusted the part, got in the car and sure enough, the engine cranked to life. He was surprised and asked the old man, "How did you know what to do?" The old man said, "My name is Henry Ford and I invented this car."

The moral of this story is that God, being our creator and designer, is in the best position to reveal our true destiny to us; and He alone knows how best to fix our lives when things seem to be going wrong.

Another way to discover yourself is by looking at those things that make you happy; those things you do for fun - things you do without anyone compelling you to do them, and those things you can do for free. For me, I like to motivate, inspire, counsel, blog and serve humanity.

Also, you can discover some traits and qualities about yourself by the positive things that others say about you. A typical example is the testimony that I shared earlier on how I was inspired to write this book through the words of one of my amazing mentors. Let me add to that narration that after having a pensive thought about the question posed to me by Ms Ecton, I asked myself: "Do you have what it takes to write a book? What will you write? How do you start?"

These and so many other questions were going through my mind. However, after giving much thought, I said to myself, "Yes, you can write a book. Yes, you have what it takes to write a book."

The point here is that I searched within myself, in addition to how my mentor saw me. I tried to ascertain what my passion was. Eventually, I came to the sublime conclusion that since I was passionate about empowering humanity, I was going to write a book on empowerment.

Being real to yourself gives you a clearer picture of who you are. It makes your life more worthy and stress-free. You will have an informed opinion about where you are headed, and how to go about it. According to Dr. Yomi Garnett, "Vision and focus are two traits that are indispensable to anyone who will be great. Today, pray that you may be given the grace to know your calling by vision, and then to abide in that calling by focus."

BOTTOM-LINE

When you have external forces propelling you to achieve success, you may go far in life, but when the force is internal, not even the sky can be your limit.

Many people only wait for external forces to inspire and guide them on the path to success. The danger here is that when you don't have that external force any longer, whether it is music, friends, money or family members, the urge to succeed may dwindle. But when your inspiration comes from within you, you can take charge of your life and your future. You are easily able to define, appreciate and inspire yourself.

The surest way to succeed in life is to discover yourself and do what you love to do. When you have fully discovered your purpose, your life will be properly defined. It's quite unfortunate that many people don't know who they are and don't take time to discover what's unique about themselves.

The starting point of the self-discovery process is reaching out to your creator for a proper understanding of your purpose - who you are and what He has created you to be. After that, you look at yourself in the mirror and tell yourself the simple home truth about yourself.

To know more about this truth about yourself, note that there are three kinds of life that people live. The first is civil life. This is the kind of life that we demonstrate before all men. Wisdom requires that we are civil to all, social to many and familiar to few.

The second type of life is the private life. This pattern of life is only visible to a closer set of people, like intimate friends and family members. By reason of familiarity, these people can say who we are to a reasonable extent. However, there is the third kind of life, which is our secret life. No one, except you and God, knows what goes on within this secret life. This is why I have repeatedly emphasized that no one can know you as much as you and God can.

So, it is in consideration of this secret life of yours – your inner self - that you tell yourself the simple truth about yourself; the truth that will determine your focus, direct your path, and dictate your pace as you journey towards actualization of your destiny.

FOOD FOR THOUGHT

It is always important for you to take some time out of your busy schedule to think about your life. You are the only one who truly knows yourself. Don't live your life according to what people say about you, or how they see you. Your primary consideration should be how you see yourself now and in the near future.

Nobody really knows your story. They might know some things about you; but they don't have the full account of your history, nor can they get the full picture of your future. It all depends on you ultimately. So, to use the words of Henry Ford, "whether you think you can or cannot, you are right"

My late father, Anthony Ukazu, would always say, "Any name you want to bear, you must work hard to bear it." Once you decide to allow many voices into your thought process, you will gradually begin to live other people's lives instead of yours. If you don't stand up to live your life, you will end up living other people's lives.

So, today, ask yourself "who am I?" "What am I created for?" "What am I passionate about?" These are the foundational questions for discovering yourself.

ACTION EXERCISE

Today, take some time and look within. Meditate and ask yourself questions about yourself. Write down your thoughts as follows:

1. Who are you and what do you think you were for created for?

2. Are you the original version of yourself, or are you living the lesser version of yourself by not being true to yourself?

3. What is the one thing that you can confidently do anytime and anywhere, and which you do not have to struggle with? (This doesn't necessarily have to be limited to any field in life. It could be just a skill or some uncommon gift).

4. Have you been able to discover your calling in life? If yes, are you striving for excellence by mastering your calling?

2

UNDERSTANDING YOUR UNIQUENESS

"If a fish is judged by its standard to climb a tree, it will forever believe it is stupid." —Albert Einstein

Albert Einstein is considered as one of the most celebrated geniuses to have traversed this world. This, I guess, is because he was able to discover himself and what was unique about him. As I mentioned in the first chapter, you cannot know or understand what's unique about you without knowing yourself.

Albert Einstein once said, "The most complicated thing in the world is tax." He couldn't understand how tax laws worked. This probably informed his opinion when he said, "If a fish is judged by its standard to climb a tree, it will forever believe it is stupid."

Interestingly, while Albert Einstein was having a hard time understanding tax concepts and their applicability, someone elsewhere was viewing tax as the most interesting profession in the world.

As rational beings, we are created in unique ways. We are all endowed with different skills, knowledge, understanding, gifts and abilities. I belong to the school of thought that believes that your gift will make way for you. While education may put food on your table, it is your talent and skill that will give you a living, if properly nurtured.

Being yourself is one of the most difficult things in the world because you might lose many friends; but in the long run, you stand to gain because it is your fake friends that will depart from you while the people who are genuinely attracted by who you are and what you do will come forward to identify with you.

DARE TO BE DIFFERENT

As a progressive human being, it is always important to strive for success. You should always dare to succeed by daring to be different in a world where everyone wants you to conform to a particular standard. According to Arnold Schwarzenegger, "The worst thing I could ever be is the same as everybody else. I'd hate that."

Being unique and knowing yourself is not very easy because every day we live our lives in the public, where we are forced to act in certain ways when faced with difficult circumstances or situations. However, it is your uniqueness that will set you apart from others. Note that circumstances don't decide who you are; they merely reveal who you are. Therefore, to understand who you are - your personality, skills, talents, and above all, your uniqueness—you have to know yourself.

Sometimes we allow our lust for possessions, power and vested interests to influence our personality. This has led many to condescend to a status that's far below their original calling. To understand your uniqueness, you need to develop a lifestyle that the world will have to conform to if they truly want to walk along the same path with you. You can't be changing or compromising yourself to suit everybody. You need to define yourself and stand by your principles. Inconsistency is inconsistent with the lifestyle of greatness.

No two human beings are the same on earth. Even seemingly identical twins have a number of attributes that are not identical. They have traits that are unique to each of them and serve to distinguish one from the other.

In my experience as a tax preparer in the United States, it's a fact that no two persons have the same amount of income in their individual tax returns. This is because a lot of factors influence the outcome of any person's taxable income, some of which are the filing status, income, applicable credits, standard or itemized deductions, dependents and other variable factors.

Dr. Yomi Garnett, a motivational speaker and author, says it rightly: "No one is quite like you in any way, even your fingerprints are unique to you, and you alone. So are your gifts and talents. Envy no one. Feel inferior to no one. You are simply one of a kind."

The quest for self-knowledge can never end. It's worthy to note that being the best in any business, academic field, or sports is quite an achievable feat. However, the main success is maintaining it. And in order for you to maintain it, the first thing is to know yourself, your passion, your talent, and what's unique about you. You will need to keep improvising new skills by training, acquiring knowledge, and attending resourceful courses. In your quest for this definite purpose of yours, you must do four things:

1. You must discover the divinity within you. By so doing, you are giving your Creator the undiluted trust to assist you in unraveling your true purpose and what's unique about you.

2. You must discover your own unique talents. Every human being has a unique talent. You have a talent that is unique in the way you express it. This means that you can do that thing in a way that no one can copy. This also simply means that each person possesses an individual brilliance that is special to him, and him alone. This means each person is basically capable of achieving something in his own way that cannot be copied by anyone else. Everyone is in this world for a definite reason, and you must be resourceful enough to discover your own definite reason.

3. You must combine the ability to express your unique talent with service to humanity. You must use your talents to fit in with the needs of your fellow human beings. That is when you will know the true essence of achievement. That is also when you will experience the true essence of life, because you have become a genuine expression of your Creator's creativity, and because you have also obeyed the injunction in the Holy Bible which says in 1 Peter 4:10, "Each one should use whatever gift he has received to serve others, faithfully administering God's grace in its various forms."

4. You must let your passion find expression. Really successful people are ruled by passion, and the reason why they are so successful is because they are following their true calling. It is this passion that allows them to be different.

MAXIMIZING YOUR ENDOWMENTS

At creation, every human being is endowed with, at least, one unique gift (which we may also refer to as talent or potential). Unfortunately, as I pointed out before, most people die without discovering theirs. To put it simply, everyone is gifted in one way or the other, but most people never open their package.

Your gift is what makes you different from any other person. In fact, Proverbs 18:16 adds a beautiful dimension of truth to this by saying, "A man's gift makes room for him, and brings him before great men."

Let me make some clarifications here. Gifts are different from skills. Skills can be learned, while talents and gifts cannot. Talents and gifts are innate potentials and they are freely given to human beings at creation; but skills can be taught and learned.

Skills often come from knowledge. And there are five different types of knowledge: Revealed knowledge, which is the type of knowledge that was revealed to those who wrote the Bible; empirical knowledge, which is knowledge based on investigation, observation, experimentation or experience, as opposed to theoretical knowledge, which is based on logical or mathematical assumptions; rational knowledge, which is the kind of knowledge that is normally used in solving rational problems like logical reasoning; authoritative knowledge, which is the knowledge one is normally exposed due to the expertise a person has attained in a particular field of life, and intuitive knowledge, which is the knowledge one gets from his innate nature which is devoid of reason or logic. It springs up spontaneously when you are faced with an unexpected situation like an accident or a crisis which needs a quick response.

As already noted, some of these forms of knowledge can be learned and acquired. However, when juxtaposed with your God-given gifts, the difference is usually clear. To begin with, you don't really have to labor to apply God's gift when the occasion demands it. Your gift will give you life and make your life much easier. It will make you to flourish where most people find it difficult to thread.

Who can disagree that two examples of outstanding talent and greatness were manifested in the lives of Michael Jackson - with his unique dance choreography; and Whitney Houston – with her unforgettable voice? The greatness that withstands the test of time involves a combination of talent, skill and originality. Mastering and merging inner gifts with acquired skills bring each person closer to their own greatness.

There's always an inherent joy when you use your talent or gift to work for humanity. According to Aristotle, "Where your talents and the needs of the world cross, there lies your vocation."

Understanding what's unique about you is very important in discovering who you are in life. When you know your gift, you will be at ease with yourself and humanity. You will be free to use your gift to solve the problems confronting humanity. According to Myles Munroe, "When you discover your gift and authority, that gift attracts people. When people come to you, they are not coming for you, but for the gift and the vision that you are serving the humanity of your generation with."

Your primary purpose in life should be to identify and use your God-give potentials, because they are closely linked to your purpose in life. Those who don't use their gifts tend to work for those who do.

Moreover, you must continually nurture your gift. When you nurture and enrich your gift with unceasing education and constant training, you will stand out in all you set your hands upon. A skill, talent or knowledge that is not constantly being improved upon will gradually become dormant.

WHAT ARE YOU PASSIONATE ABOUT?

Passion has been shown to be the driving force of success in life. Passion is stronger than power. I personally subscribe to this saying because the whole world stands still for the man who knows where he is going. A determined mind sees obstacles as opportunities and stepping stones to success; he never quits in his quest to find fulfillment in life, regardless of how many times he fails. The pessimist, on the other hand, sees failure as the end of the road.

Success-minded persons are always passionate about their goals. They never give up, and they are always motivated when they see the big picture which lies ahead of them. To them, their success and joy only become fulfilled once their dream and desires are achieved.

There is no height in life that a determined man cannot attain. Most successful people have faced frustrating situations in life, either in form of sexual abuse, financial difficulties, academic difficulties or racial discrimination before they were able to achieve success in their chosen fields. Now, some of such people have established charitable foundations. To them, this is the most resourceful way they can optimize their joy. They decided to impact the lives of others, as well as giving back to the society which has contributed to their life success in one way or the other.

What often limits us from achieving our dreams is the quality of our thinking and imagination. If we allow or cherish negative thoughts, it will be very difficult, if not practically impossible, to achieve our dreams and desires.

The Law of Attraction teaches us to always believe, think positive, appreciate and associate with whatever we like and it will generally come to pass for us. If you have a strong positive mental attitude, regardless of the negative situations that come your way, your passion and interest in life will surely serve as a motivating factor for you to triumph. As you proceed on your life's journey, your desire to succeed should always outweigh and exceed your fear for failure.

The saying that passion is stronger than power can be easily juxtaposed with the saying that love is richer than money. In other words, another way of viewing passion is to compare it with love and money in a relationship. Some people think that money is the binding factor that keeps a marriage together. But I strongly believe that love is the foundational factor that sustains a marital relationship.

Research has shown that even the many bounties of life don't guarantee happiness. Love becomes "true" not just in blissful times but in persevering through hardship. There have also been scenarios where couples have been seen living in poverty, yet faithfulness was never compromised despite all temptations.

My point is that once an individual is committed to a cause, he will pour out his love into it, nurture it, and give it his all. However, where there's no passion, it will be difficult to motivate the person.

In the labor market, employers always look for candidates who are passionate about their career paths. Some employers go as far asking prospective candidates during interviews what they are passionate about, and where they see themselves in five years. Such questions as: Why do you think we should hire you? Why did you apply to this company? etc. have strategic intents. Employers know only too well that employees will never succeed on a job they are not passionate about. The passion a person has for a job or career can make him or her work for free, do an internship just to gain experience, volunteer in the society, or serve in the community, church, association etc.

A great example of passion is manifested in the life of Dr. Michael Adenuga Jr, chairman of Nigeria's Globacom Group, who has deployed his passion for entrepreneurship to build one of the greatest mobile telephone brands on the African continent. Another example is Aliko Dangote, who has, in a period spanning less than four decades, built the largest manufacturing and industrial conglomerate in Africa, and has become the wealthiest black person on earth. Also, worthy of mention is Tony Elumelu a Nigerian economist, entrepreneur, and philanthropist. Elumelu, who rose to prominence as the Founder of one of Nigeria's largest commercial banks, is the Executive Chairman of Heirs Holdings and Founder of Tony Elumelu Foundation, an African-centered philanthropic organization dedicated to the promotion of excellence in business, leadership, and entrepreneurship across the African continent. These are people the youths can look up to and learn from their passion and skills. The impact of these people goes farther than the wealth they have accumulated. These are people the youths can look up to and learn from their passion and skills. The impact of these people goes farther than the wealth they have accumulated.

A legacy bequeathed to future generations is often the result of someone's passion and dedication. Therefore, today, I urge you to look inwards and ask yourself, What am I passionate about in life? What is that one thing I would do if I had all the money on earth or if I received no monetary reward? If identified, therein lies your passion.

WHEN TO PAY ATTENTION TO EXTERNAL OPINIONS

I gave a hint earlier that a great way of knowing what's unique about you is by observing what people often commend or appreciate you for. Humans are advanced social animals. Living and working in the society offers us enough opportunities to relate with people; in so doing, our attitudes, personalities and relationships are better discovered and shaped, in addition to our skills being honed.

Sometimes in life, we exhibit some leadership and charismatic skills that make us stand out from our counterparts without us even knowing. Some of the greatest talents or celebrities in our contemporary society were discovered when they were in their early childhood. These include Beyoncé Giselle Knowles-Carter, Shakira Isabel Mebarak Ripoll, and Muhammad Ali, just to mention a few. These individuals were spotted out by observers, friends or family members.

I have personally benefitted from people calling my attention to my uniqueness. This further manifested when I served in various leadership positions from my high school to graduate school, and even in my professional career. By virtue of making myself available to volunteer and serve at different levels, I discovered that I have public speaking skills, leadership skills, public relations skills, counseling skills, and the ability to inspire others.

However, it should be noted that not all the opinions of people matter in life. Negative minded people will want to see you fail, and as such, they will try as much as possible to bring you down by condemning, discouraging and belittling you. These are people you shouldn't listen to because they have no good intention towards you.

You must learn to exercise caution in the choice of voice you allow into your mind, so as not to be misled in life.

BOTTOM-LINE

Understanding what's unique about you is very critical to discovering who you are. In the journey of life, if you don't know where you are coming from, you won't know where you are headed.

Networking is another great way to understand what's unique about you (See Chapter 10 for more insights on networking). When you network with the right set of people, they can be instrumental in shaping not only your life, but your future. Networking has served as a veritable tool where unique qualities were discovered among people of like minds.

Volunteering in social organizations and churches can also be resourceful in understanding the capabilities and uniqueness of any human being. When you serve in committees, volunteer your time for the services of mankind and relate where needful, great opportunities may arise in addition to skills which you may cultivate in the process.

Finally, what people are saying about you and what you are passionate about can also assist you in understanding your personality.

FOOD FOR THOUGHT

There's no gainsaying the fact that each of us is unique. At creation, God created us in amazingly distinctive way. He endowed us with different gifts and capabilities which we have to use selflessly for humanity.

It's a fact that no two persons are the same. Scientists have tried to prove this in various ways, including through genetic science. Psychologists have gone a step further using temperaments (sanguine, choleric, phlegmatic and melancholic) to prove that we are all different. Theologians and philosophers also have their own opinions.

All these theories point to the fact that we all are unique in our individual ways. You were not created just to occupy space; you were not created for ordinary living; you were not created out of God's boredom; you were not created by accident or experiment. There's something special about your creation. Your purpose on earth is to figure it out and live by it.

ACTION EXERCISE

1. Do you understand yourself? Do you know what's unique about yourself?

2. What is that skill or talent that you have identified in you which depict self-discovery?

3. What are you most passionate about? What do people tell you that you seem to be very good at?

4. What is one unique trait or characteristics you can confidently be humble about yourself?

3

THE POWER OF CHOICE

In every single thing you do, you are choosing a direction. Your life is a product of choices.

—Dr. Kathleen Hall

Without doubt, we all have huge roles to play in determining what we become in life. Nobody will give you success if you don't work towards it. Regardless of external factors (which include the support you receive from friends and family) and the internal factors which motivate you to work towards your dreams, if you are not ready to walk the talk, you will remain where you are.

One of the key determinants of our lots in life is the power of choice. The choices we make go a long way to shape our lives in crucial ways. Human beings are the only creatures with the privilege of making choices on earth. This great privilege was first demonstrated when God said to Adam in Genesis 1:29: "See, I have given you every herb that yields seed which is on the face of all the earth, and every tree whose fruit yields seed; to you it shall be for food." Adam was given the opportunity to choose whatever he wanted from the Garden of Eden; he was further given instructions on how to live in the garden. He was specifically told not to eat of a particular tree. "Of every tree of the garden you may freely eat; but of the tree of the knowledge of good and evil you shall not eat, for in the day that you eat of it you shall surely die." (Genesis 2:16-17). Despite the warning, however, Adam was persuaded by Eve into eating the forbidden fruit. That was Adam's choice.

Like Adam, we all have the power to decide what becomes of us in life. We are responsible for every single decision we make, whether it is in the form of words, thoughts, actions or inactions. It doesn't matter whether the decisions are made consciously or unconsciously, directly or indirectly, knowingly or unknowingly, wittingly or unwittingly.

Sometimes, most of the choices we make are uninformed and as such we fall into the trap of making the wrong choices which, in turn, affect our lives adversely. As mentioned earlier, "One's philosophy is not best expressed in words; it is expressed in the choices one makes. In the long run, we shape our lives and we shape ourselves. The process never ends until we die. And, the choices we make are ultimately our own responsibility."

CHOICE AND SELF-DISCOVERY

Choice has a fundamental role in the discovery process and eventual destiny of any person. For instance, the choice to develop our skills and talents lies in us. Sadly, many times we fail to make proper use of this choice because we allow ourselves to be governed by the opinions of others.

Let this truth resonate in your mind always: The choice to accept who you are is yours. The choice to discover who you are is yours. And, certainly, the choice to be happy in life depends on you.

According to Albert Einstein "If you want to be happy, tie it to a cause and not to people." There are people who know that they are gifted in certain sporting, literary or recreational activities, but they allow the negative words they hear from others to sink into their hearts and dampen their enthusiasm. The end result is often frustration and regrets.

I want you to know that you have a big role to play in designing your future. Even though the society, humanity, social organizations and family can have an insight about your capability; in reality, you are the only one that knows what you can do better and best. The only role that external forces and factors can play is the one you allow them to play. You may have been told that you will be a good basketball player just because you are tall, but in reality, that may not be true. You may not even have the passion, skill, or talent for basketball.

You may have also been told that you will not amount to anything due to the poor grades you got in class or the difficulties you encountered while pursuing your education. Again, that might be false, because such persons are not the architects of your life. It is only when you allow such negative comments in your mind that your destiny could be negatively affected.

The level of success you are going to attain in life depends largely on you. The choices you make today, in addition to the amount of work you are willing to put in, will combine to fashion the cornerstones of your life and destiny. Successful leaders are not concerned about today; rather, they are always busy thinking of how they can make the most of today's opportunities to take advantage of tomorrow's possibilities.

You may have heard the saying that the journey of a thousand miles begins with a step; but I must add that it is important to ensure that the step you're taking is the right one. However, you cannot take the right step unless you make the right choice.

Yesterday is history, and can be safely regarded as gone. Today is a gift and an opportunity to leverage; tomorrow is a mystery because we don't know how it will unfold. Therefore, it is necessary that we ponder the choices we are making because our choices today will determine our eventual destinations in life.

Ultimately, we are a product of our decisions. Therefore, when faced with a dilemma, always listen before you speak, always think before you write, always earn before you spend, always feel before you hurt someone, always forgive before you pray, and finally, always think before you act. Then, act decisively, because fortune always favors the brave. And, in case you are unsure of anything, always ask questions and whenever you are in doubt do not act.

Choices are delicate because they can be decisive. So, before making any major decision in life - whether it is in business, marriage, course of study or career - make it a duty to seek the face of God. Seek for God's wisdom and direction by asking Him what He thinks. By so doing, you are trusting Him to guide you in taking the right decisions. Proverbs 3:5 says, "Trust in the Lord with all your heart, and lean not on your own understanding;"

Each choice or decision you make has a corresponding impact on your life; so, think deeply before making a choice. Some of the questions of concern that may come to your mind when making a choice are: Of what sustainable benefit will this choice be to me? Will my mind be at peace if I make this decision? Does this decision align with my goals in life? What are the risks of my options?

While pondering these thoughts, refuse to be sentimental in coming to a decision. As a general rule, it's always good to consider God first, humanity in general and then yourself. Whenever a choice is made to benefit humanity, it usually comes with a corresponding glory.

The decision we make can either make or mar us. Yet, very frequently in our lives, we are presented with choices from which we must make a decision. Add this to the cacophony of tempting and discouraging voices that we are daily bombarded with. In all these, though, we must ever be mindful of our strengths and abilities, weaknesses and limitations. These must be factored into whatever decisions we make eventually.

DESTINY MODELS

Stories abound of great people who initially faced some really difficult challenges but came out victorious, despite the many negative voices and energy they had to deal with. Examples include Steve Jobs and Oprah Winfrey.

Despite the odds which Steve Jobs faced when he was working for Apple before he was fired, he later came back and made Apple a great company. He had the choice to allow mediocrity and sentiments to becloud his memory but he never lost sight of the big picture. He knew himself and where he was headed.

The same can be said of Oprah Winfrey. She was literally told by her boss that she was not good on the screen. She was thereafter fired from her job. That was a very traumatic experience that could have made anyone to lose focus in life. But this wasn't the case for Oprah. Yes, she had the option to quit her passion to be a television personality. She had the choice of giving up what makes her happy, her passion for the media industry. She could also have allowed herself to be overwhelmed with self-pity, especially considering the depressing comment from her former boss, which could have hindered her from getting another job. But she refused to hearken to the negative voices jostling for space in her mind.

Oprah chose to follow her dreams and, today, she is regarded as one of the wealthiest and most influential women in the media industry. Her position and persistent vision as CEO of Oprah Winfrey Network has affected and changed the lives of people all over the world.

This story serves to highlight the importance of choice in our lives. You can never succeed in life if you don't make the right choices. Nothing happens by accident. Opportunities only meet prepared minds. If you have not diligently prepared yourself, even when an opportunity comes up, it will make no sense to you.

While I was at New York Law School studying Taxation Law, I initially found the major to be too complex for me, especially as I didn't have an accounting and finance background. Despite the long hours I put in daily, as well as getting tutorial assistance from my fellow students and quitting my job just to concentrate, I was still having a hard time understanding the concept of taxation. I was faced with two options: to continue struggling, with the hope that things would get better; or to venture into a less demanding graduate program.

During this excruciating period, two thoughts came to my mind. The first was: "You can never know what you know you can't know." That seemed to perfectly describe my condition. Taxation seemed to be completely beyond my comprehension, regardless of how I tried to learn. The harder I tried to understand the concept, the harder I found it hard to comprehend.

The following week, I had the second thought: "Your desire for success should far outweigh your fear of failure." This was quite positive and inspiring. So, as I said, I was faced with two options. It was up to me to decide whether to battle it out or quit the program. I decided for the first option, because I saw light and hope in it - and more especially because I believed I could make it if I worked hard and played by the rules. And guess what? I not only got a scholarship during the course of the program, but was also able to graduate with a good grade.

I told this story to illustrate how making the right choice can trigger positive changes in your life and circumstances. This is why you must think deeply about the various options life presents to you before making a decision. Failure to do this could lead to being perpetually bound by the dire consequences of a wrong decision.

TRUSTING YOUR INSTINCTS

The choices we make in our life are as a result of the thoughts and instincts that come to us. Your instinct can be safely regarded as your conscience. Without your conscience, you can be regarded as a dead being. One of the ways you can discover your true being is by listening to your instincts. Your instincts play a fundamental role in defining who you are.

Your instinct can never deceive you because your instinct is actually your intuitive spirit. It is the live wire of your existence. Your instinct influences the kind of choices you make in life. It is your instinct that tells you whether to take possession of an item or money when no one is watching you. Essentially then, if you really wish to know yourself, one of the best avenues you may want to explore is your thoughts and instincts.

Personally, I derive motivation in enlightening, educating, inspiring and orientating people. Furthermore, I have come to realize that one of my greatest strengths is helping people and putting smiles on their faces. These attributes of mine usually come up both spontaneously and in my conscious thoughts.

If truly you have been able to realize who you are in real terms, you wouldn't have much difficulty succeeding in life. This is the secret behind the success stories of most of the celebrated achievers in history. They were never discouraged in the pursuit of their life goals and dreams, regardless of the obstacles they encountered. They were not only optimistic about their future but strongly believed in the power of their instincts. They were convinced that regardless of the challenges around them, they had what it takes to triumph.

Some examples of these great leaders were Thomas Edison, who invented the electric light bulb, despite failing several times; Abraham Lincoln, who became the 16th president of the United States, after having severally failed in business, relationship and politics.

When Steve Jobs died in October 2011, Barack Obama, a former president of the United States of America, said: "He changed our thought." Indeed, Steve Jobs was instrumental in the invention of the iPhone which was a groundbreaking innovation in 21st-century communication technology. His inventive prowess is one of the most celebrated in contemporary times.

A quintessential example of someone who truly believed in the power of his instincts is the immediate past president of the United States of America, Barack Hussein Obama. The irony of his presidency is that he was the first black president in the history of the country. And he had to contest against Hillary Clinton, the wife of one of the most celebrated American presidents, Bill Clinton.

To even make it more astonishing, Obama's father is from Kenya. Moreover, he became president at a time when the economy of America had been plunged into crisis due to the policies of his predecessor, President George Bush Jnr. Yet, not only did he win the election for two term, he was also able to transform the fortunes of the country within a short time by reviving the economy and reducing unemployment rate from 7.8 to 5.5.

Indeed, Barack Obama really believed in himself; he believed that he had what it takes to lead the greatest nation on earth. He proved it by giving Americans a revolutionized healthcare system, which was tagged Obamacare. It was a feat which many past presidents, including Bill Clinton, tried to achieve but couldn't.

Obama also ensured the elimination of the then world most wanted terrorist, Osama bin Laden, who had masterminded the September 2001 terrorist attacks on the Pentagon and the World Trade Center.

One thing that can be deciphered from the lives of the two great men mentioned above and many others like them is that they never gave up on their dreams. They were not only convinced about their beliefs, passions, dreams, interests and abilities, but they also strongly believed in their instincts, which I believe was the fundamental strength and motivation they had. This should prove to you the positive power and influence that your instinct can have on your life, if only you can listen to the still small voice in you.

POWER OF DECISIONS

As I have already shown you, your life is a result of the choices you make. This means that if you don't like your present condition or the direction your life is currently going, all you need do is start making better choices.

As human beings, we are constantly making decisions that affect our lives and those of others around us. When we make the right decisions, we are bound to enjoy the dividends; and of course, when we make the wrong decisions, we are also bound to live by the consequences. As a way of advice, therefore, never make any decision when you are excited or angry.

To make the right decision, it's important to think deeply about whatever ideas or options that you have before you. To quote Dr. Yomi Garnett again, "You are necessarily a daily decision maker. This decision must be based on some information and reliable data. That is why the people around you must be wise and competent. However, after listening, you must make the final decision, as you will be the person to live with the consequences."

Daring to be different and unique in a world of "the bandwagon effect" can be tough. Choosing to toe an uncommon line or direction can be tough, especially where easier ones can be taken. It takes a courageous mind to make such a tough choice. Clear resolute decisions are core attributes of an excellent life. The world normally stands at attention for the man who knows where he is headed!

Note also that the decisions you make in life will be a fallout of your interests and commitments. The thin line of difference between interest and commitments can be seen in the values we hold dear. According to Kenneth Blanchard an inspirational author, "there is a difference between interests and commitments. When you are interested in something, you do it only when it is convenient, when you are committed to something, you accept no excuse, only result."

I have heard a lot said about destiny, including the notion that destiny is predetermined and nothing can be done about it. But let me emphasize this: The only truth about destiny is that you have been destined to make choices and to live with the consequences of your choices. So, ultimately, only you are responsible for the outcomes of your decisions. Should things therefore go wrong (which I don't pray they do), don't blame man or God but yourself!

EDUCATIONAL CHOICES MATTER!

Education, no doubt, plays an important role in the formation of our lives. Even the Bible says in Proverbs 4:13 "Your education is your life - guard it well" (GNT). One of the ways to figure out a person's passion is to observe the major he or she decides to study in college. More often than not, most students already have a feeling of what they would want to become in future. Some of them might have discovered their strengths, passions and talents in their tender years. Some go as far as prophesying who they would like to be in the future, and sometimes, these prophecies come to pass, especially when they match their thoughts and words with corresponding actions.

It's unfortunate that many people, despite having an idea of what interests them in life, still allow external factors such as the unpredictable state of the economy, especially after taking a look at how the job market swings, to influence their choice of major. Some students are pressurized by their parents to go for certain majors due to personal preferences. And then there are those who allow the opinions and decisions of their friends to influence their choice of major.

One question I usually ask any student who is struggling to decide what major to study in school due to parental or societal pressure is, "whose happiness and future is of paramount importance?" How such individual chooses to answer this question goes a long way to reveal his or her priorities in life.

Sufficient thought should be given to the major you decide to study in the university. The major must be one that interests you, and it must be one you are passionate about. If you miss the right profession for you, you might find it difficult getting back on track. But if you are able to make the right decision in choosing the major that interests you, you will not only have fun doing the major, you will get good grades when you put in the necessary amount of hard work, and you won't have much difficulty finding a job afterwards because of your skills, talents, and qualifications.

THE CAREER ANGLE

A profession, can be likened to a calling, a paid occupation, especially one that involves prolonged training and a formal qualification. A career is an occupation or profession, especially one requiring special training. It can also be taught in a formal setting like in a class or in the office setting for career advancement.

Engaging in a career that you love will go a long way to make you successful, not only because you have the skills and interest in the profession, but because of the opportunities and training you will undertake to make you more relevant and productive in the profession. A job on the other hand is a paid position of regular employment.

If you have been able to discover your gift, skill and passion and you choose a career path in that line, there's a strong likelihood that you will succeed. In fact, it is safe to categorically say that the day you discover your talent is the day you become a millionaire.

Since the career path you settle for has a lot of influence in shaping the outcome of your life, it is imperative that before you decide on a career, you synchronize your interest, skills, passion and talents with your options, to determine the best course to take. It's only by so doing that you will be able to maximize your destiny and career path in such a way that it will be productive, in addition to yielding the desired dividends for you.

One way of knowing whether you are making the right decision in your career choice (as well as other areas of your life) is to look inwards and ask yourself if you are at peace with yourself. If you are, you can go ahead with the decision. But, if your mind is not at peace, for example, if you are having doubts, it's a signal to reconsider your decision.

RELATIONSHIP DECISIONS

Another aspect of our lives in which choice plays a critical role is our relationships. Human beings are social animals. One of the cravings of humans is the need to be desired. Yet, the friends you keep can either make or mar you. They can either bring out the best in you or send you to an early grave.

Iron sharpens iron, so says the Holy Writ (Proverbs 27:17). Look at the people you associate with - your friends, associates, colleagues at work and so on. These are the persons who can easily see the best and the worst of you. They are the ones who can strengthen you when you are down. They are the ones who will tell you the truth if they are truly open and honest with you. And to a reasonable extent, they are the ones who can decide your future, apart from God and you.

No doubt, we all need relationships in our lives. These relationships go a long way to help us to achieve maximum success. According to an African proverb, "if you want to go fast, go alone, but if you want to far, go with a team."

We cannot survive in isolation. We need our fellow human beings to survive. And, as the above quote says, it is the relationships we keep that will determine how far we will go in life.

Let us see how our relationships with our fellow human beings can affect our lives positively and negatively. Let's take the relationship between two individuals, for instance. Mr. A might have been told he will never amount to anything in life by negative-minded persons or even haters, and Mr. B might have been told by mentors and other relevant individuals in his life that he will be a great man of substance.

If Mr. A finds a mentor or a great friend in Mr. C who adopts him as a partner, he can encourage him by helping him hone his skills, in addition to speaking positive words to him. These words can go a long way to shape the life of Mr. A, in addition to motivating him to be a very successful person in the society. Mr. B, on the other hand, might have met the wrong persons who didn't have informed knowledge about him and might have influenced him negatively with the wrong advice.

This illustration reflects the power that relationship can have on the life of an individual. Therefore, it is necessary for you to be properly guided when deciding your acquaintances.

The choice of marriage partner also has a lot of impact on how far you can go in life. Stories abound of successful people who have been able to attain certain heights in life, and who are always fond of saying their achievements would have been limited, if not impossible, without their spouse. No wonder the Bible says in Proverbs 18:22 "He who finds a wife finds a good thing, and obtains favor from the Lord"

Let me state it again that your relationships play a huge role in your life, and the choice of persons you allow into your life is very important because the people you associate with go a long way in shaping your life. Therefore, the choice is yours to accept circumstances that come your way, overcome them and move on.

Remember that fear can either be interpreted to mean: "Face Everything and Run" or "Face Everything and Rise." It's left for you to decide which perspective to choose and then face the outcome. I pray you choose wisely.

BOTTOM-LINE

The decision to succeed in life is up to you. The decision of discovering who you are is yours to make. Life is all about making choices. The three Ps that guarantee success in life are: Purpose, Passion and Persistence. Once you know your passion, be sure to purposefully pursue and develop it; make it your profession and persist in it. Soon, your breakthrough and success will come.

Almost invariably, we will be defined and judged by the choices we make in all areas of our lives. Your instincts, education, career decisions and relationships, all have important roles to play in the choices you make. You only have a choice on the actions you take; you dont have a choice on the consequences. So, use your power of choice wisely. Above all, it's advisable that you follow your instincts and what your conscience tells you. Every other aspect of your life can be properly adjusted once you get it right with your conscience.

FOOD FOR THOUGHT

Choice plays a fundamental role in deciding who we will be in life. The power of choice is the greatest privilege God has given to every human being. What you do with this privilege from day to day will go a long way to decide what you will become in life. This is because you are a product of the choice and decisions you make in life.

No one can help you succeed in life more than yourself. The decision is yours to make. Moreover, as you make your decisions, ensure to look inwards to know what works best for you. Not only that, in making a decision on your educational pursuit, business, career, relationship or any other major area of life, be sure to think it through, even if it takes you days to come to a sound decision.

ACTION EXERCISE

1. What choices did you make in the past that have influenced your life positively?

2. What is the one, all-important decision you are willing to take to improve your life?

3. Do you believe your instincts work in a positive way, and have they ever led you astray?

4. If there's one choice or decision you have to make to take you to the next level in life, what is it?

4

TURNING FAILURE INTO YOUR FRIEND

"Your desire for success should always outweigh your
fear for failure." —Anonymous

The desire of everyone is to be successful. Nobody wants to
fail, especially after investing time and effort in an attempt
to be successful. The irony of life, however, is that failure is a
necessary part of success. In other words, in your pursuit of a
successful life and a fulfilled destiny, you are bound to experience
failure along the way. Therefore, don't be discouraged when you
hit the walls. When you fail, you don't have to remain there. You
have to look at the factors that made you to fail and then work
towards getting it right next time.

The road to success is not straight. There will be red signals,
signifying danger; caution signs, signifying warnings; and green
lights, signifying progress. We all must experience failure in one
way or the other in order to appreciate success. Fortunately, failure
doesn't define who you are; rather it strengthens and empowers

you. So, it doesn't matter how many times you fail; what matters is that you rise each time you fail.

There's no successful man or woman who has never experienced failure in life. The difference however is that, unlike those who succumb to failure and defeat, successful people are those who have learnt to convert obstacles on their paths into stepping stones – because they understand that nothing good comes easy.

Failure plays a fundamental role in discovering your strengths and potentials. Progressive minds always see mistakes as opportunities for deeper explorations and greater discoveries. Mistakes are a necessary part of growth. So, whenever you make a mistake don't get discouraged, provided you have done all you are supposed to do. Always see mistakes as proof that you are learning or trying.

There are so many examples of individuals who have been able to tap into their failures in life and converted them to success. For example, one of America's best rap artists and producers, Aliaume Damala Badara Akon Thiam popularly known as Akon, discovered himself when he was in prison. While he was in prison, he released one of his hit tracks "Locked Up," which sold in millions. He didn't allow the confinement of the prison walls to confine the possibilities of his mind; rather he turned his failure into success.

Failure can actually be seen as success turned inside out. For you to appreciate failure, you have to think positively. You need to have the mindset of seeing failure as an experience. With this feeling, you will go back to the drawing board to ascertain what you missed or what you need to improve.

Some other examples of great people who converted failure into success include the inventor of the electric light bulb, Thomas

Edison. He failed hundreds of times before he was able to get it right.

Abraham Lincoln failed in business at the age of 22; at 23, he ran for the legislature and was defeated; he failed again in business at 24; he was elected to the legislature at 25; he lost his sweetheart at 26; he had a nervous breakdown at 27; he was defeated for speaker at 27; he was defeated for congress at 34; he was elected to congress at 37; he was defeated for congress at 39; he was defeated for congress at 46; he was defeated for Vice President at 47; he was defeated for Senate at 49; before he was eventually elected as President of the United States at the age of 51.

The question is, how many people would have continued to strive in life if they had failed as many times as Abraham Lincoln did? The lesson is, never give up. If you lose every other thing, try not to lose hope. Never succumb to failure until you have made your last attempt and never conclude that you have made your last attempt until you have succeeded.

Quitters never win, and winners never quit. So, having failed several times is not an indication that you can't succeed in life, or even be the person you were created to be. Rather, anytime you experience failure, ask yourself these questions: Why did I fail? What lessons have I learned? Am I grateful for the experience? How can I turn the failure into success? Where do I go from here? Who else has failed in this way and how can he help me? How can my experience help others from failing in their profession? In the circumstances, where did I succeed as well?

Most people bounce back stronger after each unsuccessful attempt to achieve their dreams. You may have been told that you can't succeed in life, or that you won't amount to anything in life. You may have been fired from your job. You may have experienced setbacks in your relationships. You may have failed in business, elections or examinations. All these experiences can, indeed, be troubling. However, that's not the end of life, and you can still succeed, provided you are determined to remain optimistic.

It's an indisputable fact that you can never attain true success without working hard for it. According to Jim Rohn, "Whether we are working to improve our health, wealth, personal achievement or professional enterprise, the difference between personal development, or professional enterprise, the difference between triumphant success or utter failure lies in the degree of our commitment to seek out, study and apply those half dozen things."

ATTITUDE IS EVERYTHING

Life is said to be ten percent of what happens to us and ninety percent of how we react to it. When your plans don't go as expected, the onus is on you to react positively by thinking out of the box instead of repeating the same approach or attitude that created the problem in the first place. Keith Harrell in his book, "Attitude is Everything", emphasizes the need to always think positive and maintain a winning attitude, regardless of the enormity of obstacles and challenges.

The way we see life is definitely what determines what we get out of it. According to Norman Vincent Peale in his book *"The Power of Positive Thinking,"* the best thing that can ever happen to a person is to think positive. Thinking positive is a positive way of living.

Attitude plays a huge role in our life. Our attitude to life goes a long way to influence our thinking, personality, decisions and, indeed, our general wellbeing. A common attribute of all great leaders is that they have a strong mental and positive attitude towards challenges. Regardless of the problems and stress we encounter at the workplace, school, business, and life generally, it is our attitude that makes the difference.

A person with a great attitude not only positively influences others but also uses the Law of Attraction to attract whatever he or she needs in life.

TAMING FEAR AND DOUBT

Fear and doubt are the two most negative factors that can adversely affect the life of any person. Nothing kills one faster than fear. In fact, as Shakespeare once observed, there are people who die many times before their actual death. This is what fear causes.

Same goes for doubt. With a doubtful mind, it's practically impossible to achieve success in any venture or project you are working on. The reason is simple. Doubt hinders concentration, which is essential for success. Even the Bible says in James 1:6, "…he who doubts is like a wave of the sea driven and tossed by the wind…"

Fear and doubt often paint negative images and scenarios in our minds. They are both mental impostors that make you feel you cannot achieve your dreams, regardless of how talented, skillful or hardworking you may be. Many people who ordinarily should have succeeded in life have failed in reaching their goals in life simply because they allowed themselves to be limited by fear and confined by doubt.

It's only courageous minds that can successfully weather the storms of life. If you don't have a strong and positive mindset, in addition to believing in yourself, there's a high tendency that

71

you will fail. Having courage and faith is like having sufficient gas in your car. Without sufficient gas, the car won't take you to your destination.

Again, having faith and courage is like having blood in your bloodstream; without blood, it will be impossible for you to live. Therefore, it's logical to say that faith and courage constitute the propellers with which we move forward or the wings with which we mount upward in life. When faith is lacking in your life, you are giving room for doubt to overwhelm and incapacitate you.

Doubt itself is a red flag. Whenever you are to take a decision and you can't stop doubting the rightness of such decision, then it's better not to act at all. Otherwise, you will always feel you are on the wrong side of the aisle, and you will have difficulty putting your energy into the task at hand.

How do you prevent the fiery darts of fear and doubt from penetrating your mind? By deploying the shield of faith! Ephesians 6:16 exhorts: "Above all, taking the shield of faith with which you will be able to quench all the fiery darts of the wicked one."

Of course, regardless of what your vision in life is or what God has told you to do (perhaps concerning a business, relationship, career or ministry) fear and doubt may rear their ugly heads, but if you have strong faith in yourself, your vision and most importantly, your God, then you will definitely overcome any challenges or misgivings you may have.

THINK POSITIVE, SPEAK POSITIVE

To turn failure into success, you must learn to think positive, regardless of any situation you find yourself in. You may have failed in business or have cause to repeat a class. Never allow the feeling of negativity or disappointment to knock you down. Insist always on having a strong positive mental attitude.

A natural indicator of positive thinking is positive speaking; "for out of the abundance of the heart the mouth speaks" (Matthew 12:34). More importantly, however, the words we speak to ourselves have the power to influence our life. The words you speak to yourself have power to shape your future and destiny. Here is a spiritual fact you must know: Whatever word you speak, the ground on which you are standing hears it and stamps it; the air around you inhales it and carries it as news; and thereafter the forces of nature ensure that it comes to manifestation.

Therefore, to use the words of Lao Tzu "Watch your thoughts, they become your words, watch your words, they become your actions, watch your actions, they become your character, watch you character, they become your destiny."

ACTIONS OF FAITH

I briefly touched on the subject of faith while discussing doubt and fear, but there's need to explore it deeper. Let me begin by stressing that self-discovery cannot be fully achieved without faith—faith in life, faith in oneself and faith in what the future holds.

Faith is the gas that keeps the engine of success moving. If you don't have faith in yourself, you are as good as a walking corpse. Put in clear terms, self-belief is a physical demonstration of your belief in what God has said concerning you.

Faith, above all, works on the spiritual level before it manifests in reality. According to St. Augustine, "Faith is to believe what you don't see. The reward of faith is to see what you believe."

Nothing happens by chance; you must first of all work towards your goal and believe you will be favored.

Success in life only comes to those who work hard and have a positive mind. The desire to succeed in life springs from within. You can't give what you don't have. If you don't love yourself, you can't love another person. If you don't have money you can't give out money. Believing in yourself can be likened to believing a pill will heal you if you are sick. It is not really the pill that heals you; rather, it is the faith that you have in the pill that will heal you.

Let's apply this in the spiritual sense. If you meet a man of God for healing and deliverance prayers, the prayers won't be effective if you don't have faith in the person and in the prayer; but if you have faith in the person and you strongly believe in the efficacy of the prayers, the prayers will work for you. Now, the truth is that it is neither the prayer nor the man of God that heals you; it is the belief that you have in the prayers that healed you, and that is what the Scripture says in James 2:20 "...*Faith without works is dead.*"

Faith can be likened to starting something, despite feelings of uncertainty; to take action without guarantee of success; and to persist on a course, in the face of disappointment and failure. According to Dr. Yomi Garnett, "Viewed from a spiritual perspective, faith and fear can be said to be opposites. It's also quite true what each of them brings to our lives are also opposites. Fear can lead to failure. Faith can lead to conquest." At the end of the day, it all depends on what you feed your mind with. Instead of allowing fear to rent a space in your life, make faith the landlord of your heart.

Having faith in yourself is a necessary factor for you to succeed in life. Believe in yourself. Believe you are unique. Believe no one is like you. Have a plan and work towards it while remaining focused on your goals. Soon, you will accomplish your goals and all your hard work would have paid off.

THE ROPE OF HOPE

Hope is what you cling to, while you wait for all your other investments towards success to yield the desired result. Hope is the nourishment that sustains you as you trudge the rugged road to fulfillment. However, hope can only thrive if you have discovered yourself. With self-discovery in place, it will be easier for you to hope for a brighter future. According to Adlin Sinclair, "Without faith, hope, and trust, there is no promise for the future, and without a promising future, life has no direction, no meaning, and no justification."

So, to succeed in life, you need hope. Where there is hope, there is faith, and where there is faith, miracles can happen. According to Rick Warren in his book, The Purpose Driven Life, "Without God, life has no purpose, without purpose life has no meaning, without meaning life has no significance and hope."

Hope and belief work side by side. None can exist without the other. Hope has been the bedrock of most persistent and successful people in life. A classic example of hope was displayed by former American president, Barack Hussein Obama during the 2008 presidential election, where he spoke about hope, saying, "Hope in the face of difficulties. Hope in the face of uncertainties. The audacity of hope."

Essentially, Obama, during his speech, encouraged us to always hope for a better outcome in all situations. However, he further advised that things will not get better if we just fold our hands and expect situations to change. Taking a cue from his speech,

I'll say that you cannot overcome difficulties and succeed in life if you don't work towards achieving success. You must see obstacles as stepping stones to success.

President Obama's belief and hope in the American electoral system and his vision made him the first Black American president. If you practice the law of attraction, with hope, your chances of getting your desires in life will be high.

BOTTOM-LINE

Life is not always a bowl of cherries. Even for a successful entrepreneur there are many challenges to face. No journey has ever been successful without bumps along the way. Even in the Christian life, we are taught that God did not promise us an easy road; rather, He has promised to be with us until the end of time. Simply put, nothing good comes easy in life.

For you to turn failure into a success opportunity, you need to think outside the box by having the right mental attitude. Conquer doubt and fear by always thinking and confessing positively concerning your life and destiny.

FOOD FOR THOUGHT

There is no shortcut to success. There is no gain without pain. The trials you go through in life are not designed to frustrate but to fortify you towards the accomplishment of your dream. They are meant to strengthen, not sideline you. So, always be happy when you go through trials. Your trials will either make or mar you, depending on your attitude to them.

When you fail, all you need to do is go back to the drawing board and look at what you missed and what you could have done better. Know that what really matters is not how many times you failed, but how many times you are willing to rise to the challenge by picking up the lessons inherent in the failure.

In order to appreciate failure in a positive way, don't see yourself as not being smart enough; rather, see the factor that led to the failure as an experience to learn from. Indeed, failure can actually make you to discover yourself. Most people who have benefited from failure did so because they engaged in a pensive, soul-searching process to really know what went wrong, who they really were, and if they were really passionate about the cause they were pursuing.

Only truly passionate minds can take the bull by the horn and try again, especially when they have discovered their true calling. So, whenever you experience failure, don't think it's the end of the road. Rather, see it as an avenue to revise and improvise; above all, see it as a mandatory experience that you must go through in order to attain success in life. This is how you will end up realizing that failure is actually success turned inside out.

When you fail, you learn something new, and when you succeed, you learn something new. So, you need both on your journey. Mistakes are necessary for growth. Growth is a process. One doesn't wake up as an overnight success. You will have to walk the talk.

Success is like building a house. It starts from the foundation to the roofing. A lot of process and procedures take place before it's finally completed. The amount of hard work you do in laying the foundation is not usually seen, but then, that's where the root of success is planted. No one sees the amount of work that you do silently. It's the resultant effect that is usually seen.

As a way of advice, it is always good to work hard in silence and allow your success to make the noise. No matter how sure or competent you are, it's never wise to announce your success before it happens.

ACTION EXERCISE

1. How can you inject more hope into your life?

2. Have fear and doubt had very strong influences in your life?

3. How would you advise someone who is experiencing a severe downturn in his fortunes?

4. In the light of the revelation you have gotten, what does turning failure into success opportunities mean to you?

5

UNLEASHING YOUR POTENTIAL

"He who is in you is greater than he who is in the
world." —1 John 4:4

At creation, every human being is not only endowed with some latent potent abilities but is also empowered to do amazing exploits in the world. In Genesis 1:28, God said to man, "Be fruitful and multiply; fill the earth and subdue it; have dominion…" If God hasn't embedded some potentials in you, how would He expect you to be fruitful and multiply? How would He expect you to subdue the earth and exercise dominion?

So, know for sure that God has indeed blessed you with unique capabilities that He wants you to discover, develop and unleash. There is a seed of greatness that God has sown in you that is waiting for you to nurture to maturity and manifestation. It is probably lying dormant now and may remain so until you stir it up. Paul told Timothy in 2 Timothy 1:6, "Therefore I remind you to stir up the gift of God which is in you…" The choice is yours, too, to unleash the potential in you or allow it to die inside of you (may this not happen to you!)

I said it earlier on that the day you discover your talent is the day you become a millionaire. This is because this discovery, if diligently acted upon, is sure to transform your life and catapult you to such incredible heights that your education could never have taken you. Globally, talented people are respected because they are considered indispensable assets. No employer can frustrate an individual who has discovered and developed his or her talent.

Life does not always offer us roses; in fact, it offers us more thorns than roses. It is left for us to turn the thorns to roses through the potentials that God has deposited in us. One truth you must equally note is that the world doesn't owe you anything; rather, you owe the world so much with what has been deposited in you to bless humanity.

THE COMBINED POWER OF DREAMS AND GOALS

Dream, here, refers to vision in life. Some people have great dreams; some have shallow ones; while there are others who have not taken time to develop a vision for their lives. Note however that even if you have great dreams, you won't be able to achieve them if you are not ready to unleash the potential in you.

Dreams are generally projections of the kind of life we wish to live. They may originate from personal experiences and encounters. They may come from certain happenings in the society. They may also come from direct revelation from God.

One sure way of fulfilling your dreams and succeeding in life is going beyond your comfort zone. Whatever obstacle that may be standing in your way, you stand a chance of succeeding if you dare to try. Dreams come with a creative force for them to manifest. For you to achieve your dreams, you really need to have the future in mind.

The kind of dream you have says a lot about your personality. According to Jim Rohn in his book, "Seven Strategies for Wealth & Happiness, "There are two ways to face the future, you can face the future with anticipation or you can face it with apprehension." He goes further to say, "most people face the future with apprehension as opposed to anticipation. Those who live with apprehension are always worrying because they haven't spent time designing their futures. They always live their lives trying to win the approval of someone and in the process, they end up buying into someone else's view on how life should be. On the other hand, those who face the future with anticipation have planned a future worth getting excited about. They can see the future in their mind's eye, and it looks terrific."

Goals are very important for your potentials to be unleashed. It is your goals that ignite the force in you to challenge yourself. Dreams and goals are similar but they have different meanings. Dreams can be likened to the expectations, passions and possibilities of doing something. In this context, dreams refer to aspirations and desires to achieve success in life. On the other hand, goals can be likened to something that you are trying to do or achieve. Goals are targets progressive people set for themselves in order to maximize opportunities in life. In order for you to unleash the potentials in you, your goals and dreams must be in unison.

Jim Rohn further says, "To understand how crucial goals are, observe the vast majority who do not have any goals. Instead of designing their lives, these misguided people simply make a living."

Without setting goals for yourself, it will be impossible to manage your time effectively. For effective time management, always spend time on major things. Most people spend major time on minor things, and spend minor time on major things. This is called misplaced priorities.

Socrates was right in saying that an unexamined life is not worth living. We have a high obligation to constantly remind ourselves of the purpose of our existence, so we don't lose focus or get derailed.

EDUCATION AND YOUR POTENTIAL

Education offers us many career advantages, as well as opportunities for discovering ourselves. While many people are privileged to be educated up to university level, some are not that privileged. It must be emphasized, however, that while obtaining a higher education is advisable, it is not a mandatory yardstick for discovering oneself. The most important thing is to know yourself, especially your interest and passion in life.

Formal education, in itself, is over-rated. There are many instances where the world has seen truly creative minds become more successful in life than persons who attended university. A good example is the current richest black woman in the world, Folorunsho Alakija.

Again, getting higher education is good, considering the exposure and opportunity it will afford you. So, if you have the opportunity to get one, please do. Still, I must emphasize it again that education is not a determinant of success in life.

I can show you many more examples of outstanding individuals who recorded historic successes in life, despite not attending college or being college dropouts. Their secret lies in being able to discover their calling and passion early in life. Examples of such people are:

Abraham Lincoln, a lawyer, and former U.S. president who finished one year of formal schooling, self-taught himself trigonometry, and read on his own to become a lawyer; Andrew Carnegie, an industrialist and philanthropist, and one of the first mega-billionaires in the US, who was an elementary school dropout; Andrew Jackson, former U.S. president, general, attorney, judge, congressman, who was home-schooled and became a practicing attorney by the age of 35; Justin Moskovitz, multi-millionaire co-founder of Facebook, who was a Harvard dropout. Mark Zuckerberg, also a co-founder of Facebook, dropped out of Harvard University.

Henry Ford, billionaire founder of Ford Motor Company, did not attend college. Francois Pinault, the third-richest man in France quit high school in 1947 to work at his father's lumber mill. One reason he quit school was because his classmates made fun of his poor background. Billy Joel once said, "If I'm not going to Columbia University, I'm going to Columbia Records and you don't need a high school diploma over there." He said this after learning he had fallen one credit short of his high school graduation requirement in 1967. The six-time Grammy Award winner has sold more than 150 million records worldwide.

Jay-Z (Shawn Carter) may have "99 problems," but not having a high school diploma isn't one. The American rapper, record producer, and entrepreneur is one of the most financially successful hip-hop artists in America. In May 2016, Forbes estimated Jay Z's net worth at $610 million. He is one of the world's best-selling artists of all time, having sold more than 100 million records, while receiving 21 Grammy Awards for his musical works, as well as numerous additional nominations.

Carter grew up in one of Brooklyn's roughest housing projects, dealing drugs before turning to hip hop. In 1995, Carter took his first single to Def Jam Records, the company he ended up running from 2004 until 2007. In 2008, he signed a 10-year, $150 million deal with Live Nation that gave him control over his records, tours and endorsement deals with companies like Dell and Budweiser.

Richard Branson, Founder of Virgin Atlantic Airline is the son of a barrister and a flight attendant. He dropped out of Stowe School at age 16 to start an arts and culture magazine called Student. In 1970, at age 20, he founded a mail-order record retailer called Virgin. He later opened a record shop and recording studio, which became retail chain, Virgin Records, and record company, Virgin Music. His Virgin Group empire now includes 200 companies in 30 countries, spanning airlines, music festivals, mobile companies, and other business. Today Branson owns two private Caribbean islands, Necker and Mosquito, and has an estimated net worth of $4.9 billion as of 2016, according to Forbes.

WILDERNESS BEFORE GREATNESS

I have to emphasize this point before rounding off this chapter. There is no doubt that your greatness lies in the focused, strategic and persevering unleashing of your potentials. However, you must know that before attaining your desired height of greatness, you may need to pass through the wilderness of challenges. This may come in form of antagonism, maltreatment, opposition, deprivation, disability or any other factor that is capable of discouraging you on your journey. But you must never be discouraged. You must press on till your dreams come to fulfillment.

Whatever wilderness you have to pass through in life, you have the power within you to attract to yourself all that you could ever want. I strongly believe that everybody is a potential achiever. All you need to do is never allow any temporary setback or unpleasant experience to becloud your vision of your great future. Let me quickly show you some remarkable quotes from some notable figures about the wilderness they passed through before achieving their dreams.

- I was raped at the age of 9. —Oprah Winfrey

- I didn't even complete my university education. —Bill Gate

- In my childhood days, I stitched shoes. —Abraham Lincoln

- I struggled academically throughout elementary school. —Ben Carson

- I used to serve tea at a shop to support my football training. —Lionel Messi

- I used to sleep on the floor in friends' rooms, returning coke bottles for food money, getting weekly free meals at a local temple. —Steve Jobs

- My teacher used to call me a failure. —Tony Blair

- I had no shoes. —Goodluck E. Jonathan

- I was once a prisoner before a president. —Nelson Mandela

What are you passing through now? Do not let it bother you. Things will yet turn around for the better, to yield a perfect story. I recall that during my formative years in the United States, biting words of sarcasm were used to describe my supposedly flawed writing skills by those who were supposed to mentor me. However, here I am today, sharing my experiences in a book. I repeat: There is no greatness without a wilderness. With God, your life can always be better. I believe. Do you believe?

BOTTOM-LINE

In the journey of life, you cannot do it alone. You need the support of your family, friends, community, associates, colleagues, mentors and, most importantly, yourself. However, despite all the support and encouragement you will garner both morally and otherwise, no one will have more impact on you than the motivation you decide to give yourself. Therefore, you should always challenge yourself with all the gifts, skills educational opportunities and relevant opinions which you have gained in the course of your life journey and unleash your potential for the benefit of mankind.

FOOD FOR THOUGHT

In the American declaration of independence, it is stated that "all men are created equal and endowed by their creator with certain inalienable rights, among which are rights to life, liberty, and the pursuit of happiness."

We all have potentials for succeeding in life. Every one of us is a potential achiever. We all have a burning desire to succeed in life and to make an impact; sadly, most people succumb to weakness of will and give up on their dreams too easily. To overcome this weakness, you need to challenge yourself. Your desire to succeed in life should always outweigh procrastination and unhelpful habits.

ACTION EXERCISE

1. From today, make a firm commitment to yourself that you will work towards unleashing the potentials lying within you.

2. What areas of your life do you think need to be awakened, so that your true potential can burst forth?

3. What are your dreams, goals, and desires, and how do you intend to fulfill them?

4. What is the greatest fear you have entertained, and that has prevented you from unleashing your true potential?

6

IMITATION IS LIMITATION

"Be yourself; everyone is already taken."
—Oscar Wilde

No two human beings are the same, not even identical twins. The same theory is applicable to life generally. For example, any student who wants to succeed must structure a study pattern that works best for him. If you decide to imitate the reading strategy of someone else, you are likely to hit the rocks, because your mental capabilities may differ from those of your friend or whoever you are trying to imitate. Some students just listen to their professors during class, while some will have to read their notes over and over again before they can comprehend a topic.

The same theory goes for teachers and managers. The pattern that a teacher, professor, or leader will adopt in imparting knowledge is usually different from that of others. The truth here is that there's no problem without a solution. However, if you try to unlock a door with the wrong key, the door won't open. That's how human beings are, generally. We are all created and fashioned in unique ways, such that no one can be us.

There's something unique about every living person. Discovering this unique attribute of yours can be either tough or easy. It can be tough when you try to imitate other people in discovering yourself and it can be easy when you decide to be yourself; and you can only be yourself when you tell yourself the truth.

Many people have failed in life because they tried to be like someone else. As long as you try to be someone else, you can never reach your potentials in life. In fact, you are limiting yourself and your abilities. Most times, people think that the grass is greener on the other side. We assume that life would be better if we move to a new area or get into a new relationship. Sometimes, we assume other people are better off than us when we look at their skills, talents, opportunities and personalities. This is a fallacy that arises from our failure to look inwards to see what God has blessed us with. We are blind to our own skills, talents, abilities and opportunities that we have failed to tap into.

Most of the larger-than-life figures we struggle so hard to imitate are people who have discovered themselves and understood what works for them. As humans, we always have this belief that if someone can do something, then we, too, should be able to do so. Well, this may be true, to a reasonable extent; but the greater truth is that when we try to be like other people, we have the tendency of failing, because we are not them and they are not us.

You don't succeed in life by trying to imitate others. That's an unhealthy way of succeeding in life. A healthy way of living a productive life, and which is also the best way to live life, is for you to try to challenge yourself by setting standards for yourself, as opposed to trying to compete with another person.

Let's get this right, though. There is nothing wrong in learning from others, especially using lessons from their struggles, setbacks and successes to challenge yourself to be a better person. But do not make the mistake of trying to be exactly like someone else. Competing with yourself is the key to a better life.

It is always good to challenge yourself. Change, they say, is the only constant thing in life. The change processes that take place in our lives every day can be negative or positive. Positive change comes from competing with and challenging yourself to be a better person, using a friend or a person of interest as a reference point. But a negative change is when you try to be like someone else in all totality, forgetting that you are a different being created for a different purpose.

There used to be a popular advert line in Nigeria that said, "If it's not Panadol, it can never be Panadol." Trying to be someone else is a total and complete waste of time, and does not lead to productivity in any venture you are trying to achieve.

CONSTANCY OF SINCERITY

You must be sincere with yourself and others at all times, regardless of pressures to conform to popular beliefs and fads. According to Oprah Winfrey, "Real integrity is doing the right thing, knowing that nobody's going to know whether you did it or not." Again, in the words of psychotherapist Richard Carlson, "circumstances don't say who you are, they reveal who you are."

You may be gifted in singing, entertainment, sports, academics, using rational knowledge to solve practical problems, or being artistic or creative in a particular field of life. Naturally, you will find peace in actualizing success in this career path. However, if you decide to venture into another field of life just because you think it would make your life much easier, you might be caught in the cobweb of frustration.

Of course, not everyone will like or appreciate you for who you are, but it doesn't matter. That's how life ought to be. You were created for a purpose and you have a message and a voice which the particular people whom you were created for are meant to hear. When the message is conveyed to the world, those who are in conformity with the reality and truth of your message will buy into it, because, in reality, truth normally stands the test of time.

Let me add here that you have no reason to wait to get confirmation or affirmation from anyone before you decide to be or do anything pertaining to your destiny. God is the one who created you and, as such, He's the only one who should have the final say over matters that pertain to your life.

APPRECIATE YOURSELF

Appreciating yourself is the best thing that can happen to you. If you don't love and appreciate yourself, chances are that no one will love or appreciate you.

Appreciating yourself can be summed up thus: "Self-love, self-respect and self-worth." There is a reason why they all start with 'self.' You have to love and appreciate yourself first before others can do so.

If you are not very careful, you may find yourself envying a particular endowment or talent that you observe in someone else, forgetting that you may even have better abilities than that person. Remember the parable of the philosopher who was busy trying to see what was far ahead of him that he failed to see the ditch that was in front of him. This sometimes happens to us too. We tend to focus on what is beyond us, rather than appreciating what we have deep down in us.

In business, a major strategy that a salesperson will want to use to sell his product to the public is his marketing skill. If the marketer doesn't know how to market his product very well, it will be difficult for him to sell the product. In marketing this product, the salesperson will definitely have to make it his duty to let the public know how well he appreciates the product – by telling them how unique, beneficial and, perhaps, affordable the product is.

Let's assume, for example, that the product is body lotion. The marketer will have to use herself as an example. She might even say that the reason she is looking so good is because of the product. No genuine salesperson markets a product she doesn't believe in and appreciate.

Now, appreciating yourself doesn't mean altering your physical features or chosen lifestyle to appear more beautiful and acceptable to society. It simply means appreciating yourself the way you have been fashioned. For instance, if, because you want to look classy, you decide to change your skin complexion just to feel acceptable in the society, you are not only limiting yourself but also insulting your creator and telling yourself in clear terms: I hate myself, I'm fake, I am an inferior person, I won't do better if I don't change my complexion.

The person you are trying to imitate, for all you know, might even appreciate you more than you appreciate him or her. Learn to accept your own unique qualities, whether it's your physical attributes or mental abilities.

In the course of my presentations, I often tell my audience to always try to be the best of themselves, no matter how challenging that may be. I have noticed that many female folks in the black community, especially in third world countries, tend to apply bleaching lotions to their skin in order to get a fair complexion. This indicates low self-esteem and lack of self-appreciation.

APPRECIATING YOUR ROOTS

All virtues, values and character traits start from the family. In the family, you have an identity, and you are appreciated. In your family, you have a unique voice that attracts attention when you speak. It is in the family that most personalities are built.

A good family is the greatest asset anyone can ever wish for. Apart from yourself, nobody knows you better than your family. That is why when a person decides to contest for public office, research is always done on his family background to know more about his personality and relationship with his family.

The safest haven and surest refuge any person can have on earth is the family. If the whole world neglects you and you have your family standing with you, you don't have a reason to be afraid; but if your family neglects or abandons you, then you must be concerned or learn to stand alone.

Growing up as a child in Ojo Alaba, Lagos, Nigeria, I always loved to attend St. Patricks Catholic Church and be part of the community setting where I could create strong lifelong friendships and alignments with my creator and my faith. My family members thought that I would be a minister of God, but my passion for social studies and government while in high school took me in another direction.

As I grew older, I began to involve myself in social and contemporary activities in the global world at large which eventually motivated me to obtain a bachelor's degree in Law in Nigeria. I proceeded to Law School, after which I was admitted into the Supreme Court of Nigeria after fulfilling all the requirements and subsequently, I did a postgraduate degree in Law in New York Law School. My family members weren't surprised to see the path I ventured into because they firmly supported my dream to become a lawyer, due to my strong views on truth and justice.

BE GRATEFUL

There is a later chapter of this book that is devoted to the power of appreciation and gratitude. However, I will say a few things about expressing gratitude here, especially as it relates to self-appreciation.

Being grateful for your life is a form of worship to your creator. If you are grateful for who you are and the gifts and privileges you have, you are truly on the path of greatness. Moreover, with a heart filled with gratitude, you will always have peace of mind.

Indeed, one of the potent ways of attracting blessings and more opportunities to your life is by being grateful for what you have. If you are grateful for seemingly little things, greater blessings and opportunities will surely come to you.

Permit me to share a few personal experiences with you. In my search for a rewarding and fulfilling career in USA, I worked for a security company for several years as a security officer; then I worked in different law firms as an intern and paralegal; thereafter, I worked in a consultancy company as a consultant.

Of course, all these positions were merely temporary. I was desperate for a regular job that would satisfy my career longings.

I felt so bitter and angry with myself and the society because I felt the society owed me opportunities. I also felt I was undervalued and underpaid, considering my academic qualifications and professional experience.

All efforts to get a regular job where I could work 9am-5pm proved to be a herculean task. Then I reached out to one of my mentors for advice, and he taught me about the law of gratitude. He advised me to appreciate each job I had because there were many jobless people in the society. Besides, according to him, several of my mates had been desperate to be in the USA without success.

To conclude his advice, he gave me an assignment which would transform my life. He advised me to write ten things for which I was grateful everyday. I pondered my mentor's advice and went ahead to do exactly as he had suggested. And guess what? Within a month of practicing gratitude, I found a better opportunity as a Case Manager at Sebco Development Inc., a private organization operating under the auspices of the New York City Department of Homeless Service (DHS). Interestingly, this opportunity is in conformity with my passion and interest in life.

Life can be very challenging especially when you face defeat and disappointment in life. Most people find it hard to cope with the attendant stress. I urge you, however, that whenever you experience failure or setback, try to maintain a sense of gratitude by counting your blessings. Soon, you will experience a turnaround.

Grateful beings are often successful in life. They don't complain; rather, they appreciate everything that life brings their way. Ungrateful minds, on the other hand, are complainers - always complaining of what they are yet to have. Even when their desires are met, they remain insatiable in their thought processes.

I encourage you to refrain from complaining and start appreciating life and its opportunities to their fullest.

A great way of practicing gratitude is by writing down ten things you are grateful for each morning, as you awake from sleep. Alternatively, you can decide to write five things you are grateful for once you awake, and five things you are grateful for just before you go to bed.

Being appreciative goes as far as saying I love myself, I can do it, I value myself, I like my making, I am the best, God loves me, and I will succeed. Gratitude is the internal sense of joy and appreciation that we owe ourselves and our creator. When you are grateful for who you are and what you have been endowed with, you won't try to imitate someone else. Rather, you will be concerned about being the best version of yourself.

BOTTOM-LINE

The beauty of life is in originality. You need to appreciate yourself, and your creative potentials. You need to be grateful to God and the society. You have to identify with your family.

FOOD FOR THOUGHT

Indeed, imitation is limitation. You can't be someone else; and nobody can be you. Therefore, you just have to be yourself. Anything short of this is self-limitation. And once you limit yourself, you can't perform at optimal capacity. Your talents, skills, knowledge, creativity and personality are uniquely yours. People can imitate your style, but they can't imitate your creativity. Your creativity is your trademark, and no one can take it away from you. Similarly, copying other people's style only limits your capability, whereas your creativity creates more opportunities and breakthroughs for you.

ACTION EXERCISE

1. Name one thing which is unique about you, and which distinguishes you from others.

2. What are you most grateful for?

3. Decide today that you will no longer play second fiddle. How will you do this?

4. Today, say to yourself, ten times, I love myself, I will work to be the best version of myself.

7

MAXIMIZING YOUR TIME

"Give me six hours to chop down a tree and I will spend the first four sharpening the axe." —Abraham Lincoln

One of the greatest rules of time management is to first know yourself and what you want to achieve.

A popular African adage says, "Your day starts when you wake up from your sleep." We can put it in a more concrete context by saying, "Your life begins the day you decide to start living your dreams."

There is never a convenient time to do anything in life. The best use of time comes from putting maximum value into it. It is called 'careful investment for maximum results.' Each of us has a unique biological clock which controls the peak of our productivity. The ability to know what works best for you and when you can perform best will go a long way to determine your success.

According to Brian Tracy, "Time management is the core skill of your life." Your most precious resource is your time. The time you spend on any activity determines the value and passion you attach to that project. Time can be likened to passion. I like to ask my friends, "If you would love to increase your earning capacity, and if you could do one thing all day long, which activity do you think would enable you to double your income?"

You cannot underestimate the value of time to a success-minded person. To know if you are making judicious use of your time, ask yourself if what you are doing at any point in time is of low or high priority. This will help to determine how to manage your time. In doing this, you have to bear in mind that one of the qualities of a visionary is seeing the big picture that the future holds, even while living in the present.

TIME AND LIFE

Time is the greatest asset available to mankind. Yet, it is one of the most fleeting resources. If, for instance, you lose money, friends, health or spouse, there is hope of recovery, all things being equal; but once you lose your time, you can never regain it. This is why people who are destined for greatness never trivialize their use of time. In fact, if you really want to know the thinking, priority and prospects of a man, look at what he spends his time and money on.

You may have heard of the saying, "it's either you run your day or your day will run you." You must strive to be in control of what you do with every minute of your day. You choose your day as you want it to be.

According to Jim Rohn, One of the effective ways to manage your time, is to learn to use the most powerful word in time management – NO. The ability to say "no", especially when there is so much pressure from internal and external forces, is rare and is often only demonstrated by people with a strong personality. You must learn to say 'no' if you want to make a significant impact in life. You can't just be accommodating to everybody. Saying 'yes' to everyone makes you prone to mistakes. It severely impedes your progress on the success journey.

Saying 'no' makes your life much easier, because it allows you to concentrate on the salient issues. After all, it is said that it is easier to say 'yes' after you must have said 'no,' than to say 'no,' after you must have said 'yes'.

Just as your word is your bond, so also is your time your life. According to Brian Tracy, "Your greatest asset is your earning capacity and your greatest resource is your time." Making the best use of your time is a guaranteed way of living a productive life. High productivity normally comes from consolidating your time by doing only the most important things. The difference between successful people and failures is often the fact that successful people invest their time and energy on things that add value to their lives, families and communities.

You can turn failure into success opportunities by using your time judiciously. The law of attraction teaches us that every little thing counts in life and nothing should be disregarded. It is the little things that we do that define us and also gives an idea of what we are capable of doing when faced with bigger challenges.

According to William Ballard, author of "How to Apply the 'Law of Accumulation' to Your Business and Your Life," the Law of Accumulation simply says, 'A small thing accumulated over time can become a big thing.

According to him, "Now, this principle is twofold, or is similar to

101

a double-sided coin, one side being positive and the other negative. On the positive side, if you accumulate a small thing that is good in your business, over time it will become a very good thing for your business. However, on the other side of the coin, if you accumulate bad things, or neglect several small things that don't seem important at the moment, they can become huge problems."

To illustrate this point, let's say you are a homeowner and have lived in your home for seven years, or maybe even longer. Supposing that when you reached your three-year mark, your home became not just your home but home to thousands of "demon" termites, because you neglected to regularly inspect your home for potential issues. Over time, because of this neglect, you begin to notice that your home's frame and foundation are no longer what they used to be. Now, your home is on the verge of falling apart and there is nothing you can do about it. This is the negative side of the law of accumulation at work.

We can apply this illustration to a business. Can you imagine what "little demon termites" (in this case, faulty follow-up systems, poor customer service, poor quality in merchandise, etc.) can do to your business if you leave them? If you continue to neglect them, you may eventually no longer have a business.

On the positive side, consider the methodical system of the U.S. Marine Corps. The Marines understand what can happen when neglect is permitted in their affairs. This is why they are consistently training, learning and growing. And this is why they are revered and exceptional.

The law of accumulation can apply to all areas of life, not just your business. If there is neglect in your personal, spiritual or professional growth, you can be assured that decline in these areas is sure to follow. However, if you attend to the areas that are faulty in your business or personal life, and begin to accumulate positive inputs by performing small tasks of management and maintenance, you can be assured that your home or business will be strong enough to withstand the test of time.

You can only achieve the results of the Law of Attraction if you have the time to practice the little teachings which it offers. According to Steve Jobs, "Your time is limited, so don't waste it living someone else's life."

I once read an interesting illustration that aptly highlights the value of time and why it must be properly managed and maximized. Here it is: "Imagine there is a bank account which credits your account every morning with $86,400. It carries no balance from day to day. Every evening the bank deletes whatever part of the balance you failed to use during the day. What will you do? Draw about every cent of course. Each of us has such a such a bank account, and it is called time. Every morning it credits you with 86,400 seconds. Every night it writes off as lost whatever of this you failed to invest for a good purpose. It carries over no balance. It allows no overdraft. Each day, it opens a new account for you. Each night, it burns the remains of the day. If you fail to use the day's deposit, the loss is yours. There's no drawing against "tomorrow." You must live in the present on today's deposit. Invest in it so as to get from it the utmost in good health, happiness and success. The clock is running. Make the most of today."

It's an indisputable fact of life that time management is a choice. If you decide to make time for anything, the time will always be available, but if you decide otherwise, the time will never be available. In other words, if, for example, you really wish to execute a project, you will make out time for it; if not, you will always have find an excuse for not doing it.

TIME AND GOALS

The goals we set for ourselves in life determine how we spend our time. Goals are the starting-point of time management. This means that the quality of your goals will determine your perspective of time and its possibilities. If your goals are fickle, you're bound to be frivolous in your use of time. But if your goals are sound, strategic and truly aligned with your calling in life, you will consider time an invaluable resource that must be cautiously and methodically expended.

You cannot underestimate the value of time, whether you are considering your work, business, school, relationship, or academic pursuit. Time is everything, and time is money.

Before you quit from any project you are working on, consider the amount of time you have invested in it. Always have it at the back of your mind how far it took you to come this far. This should encourage you to persevere until you break through. Don't give up on your goals. You can still succeed. All you need is to invest your time wisely on essential things like researching and mastering the art of whatever you set your mind on, because the quality of time you give to any quest or project determines the level of success you will achieve in it.

THE POISON OF PROCRASTINATION

Nothing kills a man's dreams faster than procrastination. Procrastination is simply leaving what you can do today for tomorrow; or simply leaving what you can do now for another time.

Procrastination leads to misuse and loss of opportunities in life. You may have plans to start a business, a project or even to write a book. Simply get to work on it. Delay can be dangerous. Great minds never wait for a particular time to get their work done; neither will they wait to make sure the coast is clear before they pursue their dreams.

If you wait until circumstances are favorable enough before you can begin a task, you won't ever be able to achieve anything meaningful in life. Time waits for no one. Just begin whatever you ought to do. Once you begin the task, the universe has its own way of making everything work for you, despite the challenges that might seem to be lurking around the corner.

Procrastination stops progress. The beauty of hard work is that you have a restful and joyful mind when you do the needful. So, to move up to the next stage of your life and achieve your heart desires, ambition, passion and interests in life, you must avoid the great opportunity-killer called procrastination. To use the words of Mithilesh Chudgar, "Procrastination is the grave where opportunity is buried". There are usually many more opportunities awaiting you, once you are able to complete a specific task which the universe was waiting for you to tackle.

A proven way of conquering procrastination is taking one day at a time, one hour at a time, or a minute at a time. A great way to start is doing a given task, no matter how little it may seem. As the saying goes, assuming you want to eat an elephant, you don't just eat the whole animal from every angle in one day. You start by cutting off a chunk of meat at a time and, before you know it, the whole animal is gone.

Mark Twain said, "The secret of getting ahead is getting started. The secret of getting started is breaking your overwhelming complex tasks into small manageable tasks and then starting with the first one." This is the best way to handle procrastination.

When trying to get work done by eliminating procrastination, don't overlabor yourself and don't set targets you can't reach. Be real with your ability and peculiarities. Only then will you be able to build achieve your targets.

BOTTOM-LINE

According to David Thoreau "You must live in the present, launch yourself on every wave, find your eternity in each moment." There's no gainsaying that time is everything in life and what differentiates a great man and an ordinary man is how they utilize their time. Your ability to manage and maximize time, in addition to your attitude towards life generally, is what decides whether you can rise again from any setback you may have experienced.

FOOD FOR THOUGHT

You might have had great, lofty dreams and aspirations in your early years in life. You might have told yourself that you must be a doctor, lawyer, politician or business owner. You might have even set plans in motion to achieve the dreams. However, many years after, the lofty ideas are yet to see the light of day, due to the vicissitudes of life.

Considering the setbacks you may have experienced, in addition to the time you may have invested to make your dream project see the light of the day, there is the tendency to be discouraged. Let me assure you however that it is never too late to start all over again. Your dreams will come true if you don't allow them to be killed.

ACTION EXERCISE

1. What negative thoughts are you willing to discard to succeed in your chosen field of endeavor?

2. Decide today that procrastination and fear will have no place in your life. What are you willing to do to overcome procrastination and fear?

3. Are you willing to go after your dreams, passion and calling even if you have a day to live on earth?

4. The best use of your time is now, by creating balance and investing in your future today.

8

APPRECIATION AND GRATITUDE

"The deepest craving of human nature is to be
appreciated." —Brian Tracy

The greatest joy in life is not how happy you are, but how happy others can be because of you. Everyone loves to be appreciated, loved, desired, admired, and listened to. Indeed, one of the deepest needs in human nature is to feel valued and cherished.

There's nothing that pleases a student more than getting good grades and being applauded for it. In business, the best way to get clients and customers is through referral, which is a way of telling you that your efforts at keeping your customers satisfied are recognized and appreciated. Customers won't refer people to you if they don't appreciate your work, products and services.

Brain Tracy has rightly observed that the greatest gift you can give to others is the gift of unconditional love and acceptance. The Bible emphasizes and illustrates this clearly. Jesus Christ gave His life in order for us to receive salvation. If God hadn't cherished and appreciated humans, He would not have given His only son to redeem mankind.

Appreciation and gratitude will take you far in life. When you appreciate somebody, you often try to show gratitude to them for what they have done for you; or, more importantly, who they mean to you. Great people with a noble attitude see appreciation and gratitude as a heavy debt they have to pay in life. According to Benjamin Franklin, "To the generous mind, the heaviest debt is that of gratitude, when it is not in our power to repay it."

If you truly want to succeed in life, you must learn to appreciate yourself and others. You may have faced rejection and disappointment; but you are the only one who understands yourself, your vision and your calling in life. Those rejections and disappointments don't define you when you know yourself. The disappointments and setbacks you experience are the motivating factors that will make you work harder to appreciate yourself and they will serve as challenges for you to become a better person.

Gratitude is the expression of acknowledging the oneness of the universal energy working in cooperation with your desires. Gratitude is primarily concerned with our attitude and thoughts towards life. It is an attitude of thankfulness even though our desires don't appear as we would have preferred. Gratitude takes nothing for granted, it is expressly shown with expressions of appreciation, such as "Thank you"; "I appreciate"; "I'm grateful"; "Mere words can't express my heartfelt gratitude towards you" and so on.

As human beings, we always have insatiable desires for material things as opposed to being grateful for all that we have. An attitude of gratitude causes you to be more sensitive and aware of the people around you. The more gratitude you have, the more gratitude you will express, the better and more positive your personality will be, and the higher your self-esteem becomes. An enhanced self-esteem automatically makes you become more likable by people around you.

DIFFERENT WAYS TO SHOW GRATITUDE

Practicing appreciation and gratitude can take these four dimensions, according Brian Tracy:

- Appreciation

- Approval

- Admiration

- Attention

APPRECIATION

Every time you display an attitude of gratitude by saying, "Thank you," to a person, their self-esteem goes up. They feel better and more valuable. They're even more motivated to do more of the things for which they received appreciation in the first place.

APPROVAL

The second way to make people feel valuable is to express approval. Give praise and approval on every occasion for every accomplishment of whatever size. Give praise for every good effort. Give praise for every good suggestion or idea. Especially, praise people when they do something that goes above and beyond the call of duty. Praise immediately, praise specifically, and praise regularly.

Whenever you praise people, they experience it physically and emotionally. Their self-esteem rises and they feel happy inside. More importantly, whatever you praise gets repeated.

ADMIRATION

This is expressed through compliments. As Abraham Lincoln said, "Everybody likes a compliment." Compliment people on their good habits, such as punctuality and persistence. Always try to compliment people on their accomplishments. Every time you admire something about another person, you raise that person's self-esteem and make them feel happier.

ATTENTION

The fourth dimension to gratitude and perhaps the most sought by people is attention. A way of demonstrating this to someone is listening to them patiently, quietly, calmly, thoughtfully, and without interrupting. According to Steven R. Covey "Most people do not listen with the intent to understand; they listen with the intent to reply."

Gary Chapman in his book, "The Five Love Languages," emphasizes that, as humans, certain things make us feel loved, depending on our unique traits. According to him, the five love languages are: Words of affirmation, physical touch, gift, services and time.

I quite agree with Mr. Chapman's observations because as human beings, we respond to situations and stimuli in different ways. And, it is advisable in our daily relationship with individuals, that we know what works for them and how to relate with them.

No matter what your condition may be, always be grateful for all of your senses, for the miracles of sight, sound, touch, taste, smell, and feeling. You can be thankful for the functioning of your body and for the health of your limbs. You can be grateful for the incredible gift of the life that you have lived up until now, and the great life that lies ahead of you. Think about your current blessings and reasons to be truly grateful.

Develop an attitude of gratitude and practice the four As to show your gratitude towards your loved ones, coworkers, and employees.

PRACTICING GRATITUDE 101

A very important key to success in life is to practice gratitude. Practicing gratitude entails accepting in totality whatever circumstance you find yourself. When you practice gratitude, you are telling the universe and God, I thank you for what you have placed in my life. It is good to appreciate even humble beginnings, and it's always important to celebrate little successes. It is in little acts and deeds of this nature that great opportunities and strides come to us.

There are so many things you can appreciate God for. As human beings, we tend to take so many things for granted. These include the air we breathe, the clothes we wear, the accommodation we have, the food we eat, the job we have, the education we have received, the families, friends and opportunities that have come our way. Most times, we take these things for granted, forgetting that, elsewhere, somebody is craving and begging for mere survival.

Some people are finding it difficult to breathe, and have to depend on oxygen-mask for survival. Some people are feeding from waste bins, while some people don't have access to potable drinking water. Some persons are looking for the clothes you use as rags.

Sometimes, we complain about our jobs because we think we deserve better positions or payment. However, somewhere, somebody is looking for any job just to be able to foot his bill or to put food on his table.

A life filled with appreciation is a life of testimony and happiness. As mentioned and advised earlier, everyday write 10 things you are grateful for. Do it for a period of three to six months and see the level of improvement and success you will attain.

Today, I charge you, appreciate your challenges because they are part of your growth process. The teaching and practice of gratitude is practically synonymous with the teaching and practicing of humility. Gratitude teaches us humility. Gratitude teaches us to always appreciate every good deed, no matter how little it is, while making us accept challenges and trials as part of our growth process.

Personally, gratitude has made me an enthusiastic and positive minded person. It has allowed me to focus only on the bright side of life and it has totally changed my perception, attitude and understanding of life.

There is a story told about a professor who gave an unannounced test to his students. The professor gave each student an empty sheet of paper with only a tiny dot in the middle of the paper, and asked them to write what they saw on the white paper.

The students were perplexed as to what to put down on the paper. At the end of the test, the professor reached out to the students individually to see what they had written. Without exception, they each described the dark spot and ignored the white paper itself.

In reality, that is how most of us view life. We are so fixated on the negative side of life that we fail to see the good health we have, or even the jobs, education, knowledge, understanding, love and care we get from family and friends. We are more concerned about other opportunities we are hoping to get, believing that the grass is greener on the other side. We fail to understand the simple fact that our life is a gift from our loving and caring God. We also fail to understand that, if we look inwards, we will always have reasons to celebrate.

Here, I will further show you seven gratitude habits that can guarantee you a fulfilled life.

1.   Have a daily gratitude book: This simply means that you have to be grateful for every second, minute, hour and day you live on earth. Be grateful for the air, food, opportunities, friends, and even challenges that come your way daily. Count your blessings and write them down.

2.   Neutralize the difficulties of each day with gratitude: As human beings, we face disappointments and challenges daily. The best way to neutralize the negative feelings that come with such challenges is by recounting and appreciating all you have been able to achieve that day and all that worked in your favor. By so doing, you will realize that the day has not totally been unproductive and negative.

3.   Overcome hatred with love: Love, indeed, is the only thing that can counter hate. As humans, we always have a tendency to feel bitter each time we are hurt. This feeling might result in a lasting hatred for the offender. But then we must know, as rational beings, that having grudges against another will not change anything; rather, it will increase the hatred. But when you insist on seeing the good side of the person, you will know that you have a lot to gain from the person despite the anger the person may have caused in you.

4.   Replace criticism with gratitude: The opposite of gratitude is complaining. Grateful minds don't complain. Married people sometimes criticize their partners as opposed to being grateful for the positive qualities they possess. Instead of criticizing your colleague or partner, insist on appreciating that person.

It's instructive to note however that criticism is not always entirely wrong. According to Uche Okorie, a maritime lawyer, "When you are criticized objectively, examine it. If it is untrue, ignore it. If it is unfair resist the temptation to be irritated. If it is ignorant, just smile. If it is justified, then it is NOT criticism, LEARN FROM IT!"

5.   Be grateful for your challenges: It is certainly true that when one door closes another one opens. Besides, it is said that anything that doesn't kill you will only make you stronger. Whenever you experience setbacks in life, rather than cry over spilled milk, use the opportunity to think out of the box. Grateful minds always see challenges as occasions to embrace new opportunities. No problem will come to you that you can't overcome. Challenges are stepping stones to greater heights, if only you can think positively. But if you cloud your mind with negative thoughts, your challenges will mar, instead of making you.

6.   Always express heartfelt gratitude to everyone: It is an indisputable fact of life that we all need to depend on others for assistance in one way or the other, just like every single part of the human body plays a vital role in the life of every person. I encourage you to appreciate everyone you meet on the journey of life because they all have a role to play in your life. No matter

116

the role they play in your life, make it a habit to say "thank you". Don't take little deeds of kindness for granted because it's from the little deeds that mighty deeds and opportunities come through. Most importantly, remember that happy people are not the ones who become thankful people; rather thankful people are the ones who become happy people.

7.   **Appreciate and focus on what you have:** Appreciation is the highest form of gratitude. Appreciation entails being happy with what you have, and being satisfied with all you have in your possession. According to R. H. Bradley "The secret to happiness is to admire without necessarily desiring." On his part, Dr. Yomi Garnett says, "Contentment makes a poor man rich, while greed makes a rich man poor."

I urge you to always appreciate everyone in your life; appreciate all you have; be satisfied with all you have; and never be jealous of the property of another.

Let me reiterate that the more you focus on gratitude, the more you will appreciate your life and the happier you will be. An appreciative attitude will bring you into more conscious awareness of your blessings and prevent you from taking them for granted.

GRATITUDE, DESPITE DISAPPOINTMENTS

According to Rumi "Don't grieve for what doesn't come. Sometimes, some things that don't happen keep disasters from happening".

Below are some of the negative energy we receive when we allow circumstances to overwhelm us and deprive us of a sense of gratitude:

1.   **Faultfinding:** Grateful minds don't complain neither do they find fault, rather they appreciate whatever life brings their way; knowing fully that one of the secrets of success in life is the thoughts we allow into our mindsets. Once you occupy your mind with negative thoughts, negative thoughts will manifest in your life. So, always learn to see the good in others.

2.   **Complaining:** Over time, I have learned to accept whatever comes my way as opposed to complaining. Nobody likes to associate with anyone who complains and anyone who likes to explain with excuses. A great factor responsible for complaining is the ego. When your ego is at play, it will make you feel you deserve more and that you have been shortchanged. Once this feeling rears up its ugly head, pride comes in and makes you feel you have been relegated. Men with ego tend to feel they are superior beings. This makes them have denigrating attitude towards their fellow men. Complainers always love to complain. They are never satisfied; they are always thirsty for more luxuries. The more you practice not criticizing and not complaining, the more your mind will be filled with thanksgiving and appreciation.

3.   **Taking the seemingly little for granted:** As rational human beings, no human being is indispensable; no part of the human body is indispensable. They all have specific roles to play in the emancipation of the humanity and the human body. For example, the excretory part of the human body is so little, but very effective. If it decides to shut down, the body system will be restless and the human anatomy system won't be able to function in an optimal capacity. In the same vein, we take so many things for granted such as our five senses and the air we breathe. We also take people in our life for granted forgetting that it is always good to celebrate humble beginnings.

DEALING WITH REJECTION

One of the most devastating of human feelings is the feeling of rejection. Nobody likes to be rejected. Everyone likes to be appreciated. The opposite of appreciation is rejection. While appreciation is synonymous with gratitude, rejection is synonymous with ingratitude.

Once you feel rejected, the experience can have a negative impact on your life and severely impair your perception of life and of yourself. However, if you truly know yourself, in addition to knowing your calling, rejection can never hinder you from fulfilling your destiny. As the Scripture clearly affirms, "He who is in you is greater than he who is in the world" (1 John 4:4). Rejection is not for true children of God because God can never reject any of His children. We are divinely configured to achieve wonders, whether people appreciate us or not.

Whenever you are faced with rejection of any kind, all you need to do is look within yourself and tell yourself, "I am a winner, I can do it, I am the best." Things might not be working well for you right now, but you must keep believing that better days lie ahead. Regardless of how many setbacks and rejections you have received, always keep your dream alive and tell yourself daily that God is always with you.

A healthy way of living through rejection is to think of how you started, how far you have come in life, how much potential you have in you and how much you owe the world to succeed and be a blessing to others. What makes an individual stand out from his peers is his capacity and wisdom in dealing with the trials, temptations and setbacks he faces on his journey to finding purpose and meaning in life. This is what makes great men to stand out and serve as mentors and leaders.

That said, I must also add that rejection, just like failure, is inevitable in life. Not everyone will like you or appreciate your way of doing things. However, you must never allow rejection to define you or impede your progress. As Maya Angelou once said, "We may encounter many defeats, but we must not be defeated."

Having an ideology that can serve as a motivation whenever you experience low moments, such as in times of rejection, it helps to keep your spirit and hope alive. Your decision not to allow failure and frustration to overrun you, and your strong determination for success are mindsets that can help you surmount challenges as they come your way.

Note it once again: Rejection and failures have a role to play in your life. If you know yourself, you will learn not to be bothered about what is said about you.

BOTTOM-LINE

After self-discovery, the next necessary step is self-appreciation. Appreciation is the sublime acceptance of the reality of whom you are, and it signposts originality. It is also reflects the value you place on others and the opportunities that life brings to you. Gratitude, on the other hand, is the outward demonstration of appreciation through words and deeds.

The more you focus on appreciation and gratitude, the more you will appreciate your life and the happier you will be. An appreciative attitude will bring you into more conscious awareness of your blessings and prevent you from taking them for granted. Remember, the happiest people are not necessarily the ones who have the best of everything. Rather, they tend to be those who are grateful for everything they have.

As Whitney Houston said, "The greatest love of all is happening to you now. The greatest love of all is inside of you."

Remember also that rejection is the opposite of appreciation, and be mindful not to allow it alter your dreams. Take all these to heart and see how your personality takes a new look.

FOOD FOR THOUGHT

Every human being likes to be happy. The feeling of happiness comes with satisfaction, contentment, and joy. When you begin to have internal joy and fulfillment, it means you are in alignment with your true self and the real essence of your creation. When you see yourself achieving some feats with relative ease and getting approval from people at your place of work, school, business or community, there's a high tendency that you are impacting positively on the lives of the people around you.

To gain happiness while practicing gratitude and appreciation, always channel your energy towards good causes rather than material things of the world. I say this with all sense of responsibility knowing well that it is the little things of life that matter. Essentially, the three basic human requirements for happiness are: something to do, something to love and something to hope for.

ACTION EXERCISE

1. What is the greatest factor responsible for your lack of belief in yourself? Describe an incident that reinforced this.

2. What inspires your belief in yourself? In the past, what made you overcome your lack of confidence?

3. What can you do today to jettison memories of rejection and bring forth appreciation?

4. What vital lessons have you learned from rejection?

9

THE TONIC OF MEDITATION

"Silence is the element in which great things fashion themselves together." —Thomas Carlyle

Your journey to success cannot be complete without the practice of meditation. Meditation is an earthly practice with a heavenly experience. While human beings relate to God through their prayers, God communicates to human beings through meditation and prayers. Through meditation, we allow ourselves, as creations of God, to become witnesses to the revelations of God's everlasting work.

According to Wayne Dyer an inspirational author, "meditation is simply the act of being quiet with yourself and shutting the constant monologue that fills the inner space of your being. It is stopping the constant bombardment of thoughts and the seemingly endless chatter filling your inner world which prevents you from knowing your highest self". With the proper application of meditation, you will be better poised to know what you should be doing at any particular point in time.

When you meditate, your brain stops processing information as it normally would. During meditation, your pensive mood gets activated, which enhances your discerning ability. With meditation, you see life from a different perspective. Moreover, you develop a unique understanding, as well as an appreciation of beauty, nature, and humanity.

With meditation, you gather strength, knowledge, wisdom and understanding to deal with life situations and challenges. You also achieve anger control, stress reduction, fatigue reduction, amelioration of health-related challenges, in addition to the creativity it will inspire in you.

Meditation plays a fundamental role in discovering who you really are. You create your life with your thoughts. Your mind is constantly shaping the world around you. Meditation is not all about thinking, but it's about reasoning and perception. It gives you a bigger and larger picture about life.

According to Dr. Yomi Garnett, a motivational author and speaker "No one can truly access his higher self without the practice of meditation, which involves intense concentration on a word, prayer or scripture to the exclusion of all other thoughts. The mind experiences abstract level of the thinking process and ultimately transcends to the state of pure awareness. It is during meditation that subconscious activity is at its peak, making it the most fertile ground for planting prayer. During meditation, blood pressures comes down, stress is alleviated, while insomnia and anxiety are relived. Also, because of increased brain wave activity, there is increased attention span, creativity and learning ability. Finally, the effects of meditation last into your daily activity and you become a calmer and more serene person."

The part of the brain that plays a huge role in mindfulness is the frontal lobe of the brain. That is the part of the brain that is responsible for reasoning, planning, emotions and self-conscious awareness. It should be noted that while all reasoning is thinking, not all thinking is reasoning. The distinction between reasoning and thinking is the thin line that makes the difference in meditation. That's why the Bible in Proverbs 4:23 says "be careful how you think, your life is shaped by your thoughts" (GNT).

WHAT REALLY IS MEDITATION?

Meditation is a metaphysical spiritual exercise. Generally, it involves concentrating on a particular word, Bible passage, or sentence, as the case may be to the exclusion of all other thoughts. It can take different forms, depending on what a person wants to achieve.

Meditation helps us to examine ourselves. As Socrates stated, "an unexamined life is not worth living." No wonder, meditation has been described as the food and oil of great men. There's no great man who doesn't meditate.

Meditation can be done anywhere and at any time. All it needs is absolute concentration and silence. Meditation helps you to assess your strengths, weaknesses, abilities and intuitive capacity. Our body system cannot function very well if we are not relaxed, neither will it function well if our thoughts are scattered. So, it's imperative that we meditate every day.

You discover and comprehend yourself and others better when you practice the art of meditation. Even if you can't practice meditation for thirty minutes, you can start with three or five minutes and gradually build it up. The act is simple. Just take out a little time during the day, and reflect on a particular word. Allow your mind to be open. Thoughts will flow in naturally when there's little or no distraction, and it's in that state you gain insight to life in addition to relaxation.

Three types of meditation have been identified.

1. GUIDED MEDITATION

This is a form of meditation in which a student is taught by a master or a superior in the art. This meditation process can be likened to a master-servant relationship. The master teaches the student what he needs to do to be progressive in the meditation process. This is similar to when a doctor advises his patient on health-related issues, or when an attorney advises and counsels his clients on legal issues.

We can take this form of meditation as the one that exists between us and God. For you to discover who you are, you must reach out to your creator who will guide you in discovering your authentic being.

2. SENSORY MEDITATION

As the name implies, this involves the use of the senses. At creation, we were all created with five senses: taste, sight, touch, smell, and hearing. Basically then, this type of meditation is done when you use your sense organs and you focus your attention on what you are doing to the exclusion of what is happening in the world.

As a student seeking to succeed academically, discipline is what helps you practice concentration. You cannot achieve success in any field of life without discipline and concentration. Meditation works with concentration. You need to pay detailed attention to your present sense environment. Meditation works closely with our senses. When you concentrate your mind and thoughts on a particular word or thought, your whole body is fixated on it, and in turn you get a deeper meaning to it.

3. MOVING MEDITATION

This form of meditation is also called mindfulness meditation. You can practice this form of meditation carrying an object in your hands and concentrating on it. Your whole mind will be focused on this object. The focus of this meditation is the mind itself. To attain a perfect state of health, one has to remain mentally calm, steady and emotionally stable.

In a nutshell, meditation makes you a better and transformed person. When you practice meditation, your attitude to people and life, in general, changes for the better. Irritable actions and situations are greeted with affectionate love and emotional goodwill.

When meditating, you are detached from the realities and problems of the world, and this not only makes you appreciate where you are, but who you are.

The direction of where of your life is headed can be better understood when you meditate. Before you begin any journey, you stand a chance of moving in the wrong track or direction if you don't have an idea of where you are going. When you meditate right, you get insight into where you are and where you should be heading.

With the proper application of meditation, you stand a better position to unravel the mysteries and myths surrounding not only your problems, but also those of the world and humanity

127

in general.

Meditation is not a difficult task to undertake, and you don't need to have all the time in the world to meditate. All you need is determination, because if you are determined to do any task, nothing will stop you.

Contrary to what many think, meditation is not reserved for a particular set of persons such as monks, theologians, teachers or leaders. It is meant for every person. Just as other skills are learnable through practice, meditation becomes a way to daily refinement.

One skill is enough to change your life if properly applied. A creative skill can account for ninety percent of all your life income or success in life. If you are looking for such a skill, meditating is the right way to start. Meditation doesn't involve much time if you want to do it. If you have time to get your hair done, or use moisturizer among hundreds of other anti-aging techniques, then you have the time to meditate. If you have time to exercise five to thirty minutes daily, you have the time to meditate. If you have time to watch soccer, entertainment, or even engage in any leisure activity, then you have time to meditate if you want to.

BENEFITS OF MEDITATION

You cannot underestimate the power of meditation in the life of any success-minded person. According to Yomi Garnett, "One of man's greatest failings is his inability to sit alone by himself, to engage in the deeper activities of contemplation and meditation. Today, commit some time to sit and think. Meditate. This will give you access to the flow of divine wisdom and insight."

Meditation is one of the best things that can ever happen to any person. If one-third of the world's population practices meditation, the world will be a better place to live in. There will be peace, tranquility and understanding which the world currently lacks. With proper application and the precise use of meditation teachings, our psyche, orientation, perspective and understanding changes. This is because, one of the most valuable things we can get from the practice of meditation is an understanding heart. And with an understanding heart, you will have a harmonious heart filled with tolerance. With an understanding heart, humanity will experience true love, peace and a blissful relationship. The goal of meditation is for a peaceful heart, and it is one which can lead to true usefulness.

Meditation has a process. You have to know what it means to meditate, and how to meditate before you can fully engage in the practice and in turn reap or enjoy the benefits inherent in it. Meditation can be safely regarded as the food of the human soul. Our human spirit, soul, body and mind need meditation to stay alive. Meditation makes us more rational balanced human beings.

BETTER FOCUS

With meditation, you get a clearer picture about life on the larger scene. Meditation helps to bring about alignment with humanity. It affects your interaction and relationship with people who may have separated from you in the past due to disputes and misunderstanding.

Many of the separations that have taken place in life are partly because of fractious attitudes which meditation could have fixed if utilized. The understanding and proper communication that is lacking in human relationship can be achieved with meditation.

Meditation helps us to better focus and assists us in understanding things for what they are. Moreover, it gives you direction as to what you should be doing in life. For example, you are able to understand whether you should be playing soccer, basketball, or teaching.

Meditation is like the lens and retina with which we see. When you have a proper understanding and vision of any object, situation, or problem, you will be better poised and focused to address any challenge or difficulty that may result from it.

Generally, when you are focused in life, you get more energy, determination and an optimistic spirit to achieve whatever you want. The energy that comes to your will is very powerful when you practice meditation. With meditation, illusion and reality are separated.

LESS ANXIETY

According to Francis De Sales, "Where there is peace and meditation, there is neither anxiety nor doubt." Nothing worries the heart of a man more than the fear of the unknown. However, allowing this negative energy in our lives can hamper our performance and progress in life.

To have a settled and relaxed mind is one of the most precious virtues and gifts much needed in the world today. Meditation helps you to feel lighter by untangling the loads of problems you may be facing. With effective practice of meditation, you will always find it easy to overcome your challenges. Of course, the challenges may not immediately disappear but they won't bother you as much because you have a better view of them.

ENHANCED CREATIVITY

One great benefit of meditation is that it helps to improve your concentration levels, which in turn will make you more creative and productive. Creativity is the beauty of life. Creativity rules the world. No skill, talent or academic achievement has empowered any soul more than creativity. With creativity, your instincts come up with new ideas.

When you meditate, you clear your mind of distractions and instead focus on the act of meditating itself. Meditation serves as a balancing factor between your inner and your outer world. Your spirit and instinct might be disposed to a decision, but your flesh might be uncomfortable with it. When this conflict appears between your inner and outer beings, this is where the application of meditation comes in to strike the balance.

Meditation helps you to connect with your innermost being and your creator. Meditation gives you wisdom which helps you see the future, in addition to making your life easy.

BETTER MEMORY

You may have experienced an ugly past that still haunts your mind today. I can assure you, however, that with the proper application of mediation, you can eliminate any negative ideas and memories. Meditation helps you to think in the present as opposed to dwelling in the past.

The words that you hear from people around you can affect your state of mind. They can either give you peace and joy, or create disturbance (such as jealousy, anger, frustration or sadness). You're affected because your mind is not concentrating on the positive.

131

It is wandering, with so many thoughts jostling for your attention. Meditation is the key to control 'emotional pollution.' Note that if you are unhappy or depressed, you are not the only one being affected; you are equally spreading the negative feeling to the entire environment.

The silence of pure awareness which is obtained from meditation is extremely refreshing to the mind; consequently, it finds it increasingly easy not to cling to old thought-patterns. Rigid and unhealthy habits of thinking and feeling begin to fall away of their own accord. When this happens, the mind is actually learning to heal itself.

Meditation helps to improve memory, self- awareness, tolerance, empathy and goal-setting. Our human memory cannot function efficiently and effectively if our memory capacity is not well balanced and structured. One of the great ways our human memory can function very well is with the practice of meditation.

LESS STRESS

Meditation takes us from a busy lifestyle into a more reserved place of solitude, giving our body a very deep level of rest. Rest is how the body heals itself, which it does by throwing off the stress, fatigue, and toxins accumulated during our daily life.

You need good health to succeed in life. Meditation helps to balance your health. It is said that all illnesses begin from the mind; so, by attending to the mind, clearing it of any disturbances, the healing and recovery process is accelerated.

Norman Vincent Peale an inspirational author, rightly said, "Learn to relax. Your body is precious, as it houses your mind and spirit. Inner peace begins with a relaxed body."

Let me share a story I heard some years ago on this. The story is about a sick mother whose son was a doctor. The son gave the mother a pill, but she refused and insisted she needed an injection. The son told the mother that as an experienced physician who had been treating different patients for years, he was sure of the prescription he was giving her. Still, the mother refused to take the pill and insisted she needed an injection. According to her, she had seen him injecting other people, and they got well.

After some pleading, the mother agreed to take the pill. Sadly, even after then, her condition didn't improve. When the son realized what was going on, he decided to inject her with only water as a placebo. In two days, the mother's health dramatically improved. This is an example how the root cause of an illness may lie in the mind or belief.

My family used to own a hospital, and each time I visited the hospital, I heard music in the background. I wondered why music was played in such silent and melodic tones. I later understood that the music was a form of spiritual and faith-based healing method. When patients heard the spiritual healing music, it gave them hope of survival.

Really, many of the deaths that occur daily are due to the high levels of stress that people go through. By practicing meditation, stress, worry and anxiety depart from our lives, paving way for a positive state of mind, which has a positive impact on our physical, emotional and spiritual well-being.

Other health benefits of meditation, aside from stress reduction, are better sleep, lower blood pressure, improved cardiovascular function, improved immunity, and restful mind in the midst of all the turmoil that's going on around you.

Meditation helps you do less and accomplish more. The practice of meditation brings coolness to the brain. The more we meditate, the less anxiety we will have, and it turns out this way because we're actually loosening the connections of particular neural pathways.

ANGER REDUCTION

One of the most powerful effects of meditation is anger reduction. Whenever we are angry or provoked due to stress, we have a tendency to react. However, with the practice of meditation, anger can be reduced. According to Yomi Garnett, "anger, like dynamite, is a potent explosive. Unless it is handled with wisdom and self-control, it can precipitate devastating damage. If you allow your temper to get the best of you, it will only reveal the worst of you."

BOTTOM-LINE

Meditation gives us an insight to life. Meditation can be described as earthly prophecy and revelation. When you practice sensory and moving meditation, many benefits come with it, such as better focus, less anxiety, more creativity, better memory and less stress. Meditation unravels issues surrounding problems and concerns. If you really want to unravel the mysteries of life and your personality, the practice of meditation will be a good place to start. My meditation coach, Georgina Galanis, says it better: "Meditation opens spaces in your mind between thoughts, and allows the silence of creation to flourish in your life. It is up to you how much you fill up your sky or allow space so you can fly freely".

FOOD FOR THOUGHT

In the words of Bruce Lee, "as you think, so you shall become." Meditation is a way and a pattern of life which everyone ought to adopt for effective living. Meditation is merely an abstract relationship with the innermost body through a present mode relationship. Meditation takes different forms. You can sit down quietly, folding your hands and legs in akimbo mode. It can also be practiced using symbols or fixing your minds on a particular word or mantra.

Meditation is not hard to practice. Starting gradually is all that is important and you can always build on the strength and achievements that will come along with it.

Meditation gives you peace of mind. Your peace of mind is very important to live healthy. When your mind is at peace with your job, friend, spouse, decision, association, family, or any particular situation in which you are into, you will definitely be at ease. This is because your highest self wants you to be at peace.

It is very important whenever you are about to act, always ask yourself this question, is what I am going to say or do going to bring me peace? If the answer is no, please reconsider your position on the issue. Whenever you are in are in dilemma about any situation, two voices are always are at play. It is always advisable to listen only to the voice that gives you peace of mind.

ACTION EXERCISE

1. In real terms, what does meditation mean to you?

2. Have you ever practiced meditation? If yes, what kind of meditation did you practice? What is your favorite style of meditating? How long and how often do you practice meditation?

3. What has been your experience with meditation? Was it beneficial to you?

4. Describe what happens in your meditation. Does the practice of meditation change other areas of your life? Describe how.

```
┌─────────┐
│   10    │
└─────────┘
```

REACHING OUT

"I am because of what other people have made of me."
—Ubuntu – African Proverb

As social animals, we live in an earthly community that can be conveniently called 'the global village'. This provides us with another great path to self-discovery - reaching out to the global community through service.

We relate with our fellow human beings every day in different capacities. Each relationship we have does not only define our being but leaves a lasting legacy in the mind of the other person. Your human relationships can actually be some of the greatest defining moments of your life.

Reaching out to the world can take different shapes and forms, depending on the issues at hand. According to Samuel Johnson, "Knowledge is of two kinds, it's either you know the answer or you know where to find it." Some people discover hidden strengths and qualities when they make themselves available for service to humanity.

You may have been able to affect the lives of people within your community by the way you advise or solve the problems of others. Many people have been able to discover their talents through performing or showcasing their skills during concerts, exhibits, social gatherings or fundraisers. All these activities help to discover true potentials.

No one exists in isolation. This truth is captured in a famous African saying, "Ubuntu" (which translates as "I am because we are, I am because of what other people have made of me"). It basically means that we all need each other to survive. It is this interdependency that makes our lives more beautiful and meaningful, since the strength of each person makes up for the weakness of the other. This is the reason why there's separation of powers in government and division of labor in corporate organizations. This division merely helps to strengthen the expertise of any one person and creates a whole new perspective with a fusion of multiple talents and skills.

Focusing on a particular area of life makes you more detailed and result-oriented as opposed to being a "Jack of all trades, master of none". You have greater chance to achieve maximum success when you focus on one particular area of life, while also reaching out to others because you just can't do it alone.

LEVERAGING ASSOCIATIONS AND NETWORKS

Association and networks influence your life significantly. Influence doesn't just happen. It builds up gradually, through constant interaction. To understand the role of association and networking in human life, the words of ancient Greek philosophers, Socrates and Aristotle, come to mind. According to Socrates, the human mind is usually blank at birth, and it is the society that decides what becomes of this mind through association. Aristotle, on his part, said, "no one is born immoral, it is the choices that we make after birth that make us either moral or immoral."

There is no doubt about it. Association leads to adaptation. The people you spend the bulk of your time with and the environment you relish will have a major influence on your character and attitude to life. Put simply, the company you keep plays a huge role in the kind of person you become and reveals your chosen moral standards. You mirror the people you spend most of your time with. If you associate with liars, ignorant and uninformed people, you will gradually begin to think and act like them and, unless you are able to separate yourself from them, your level of awareness and objective in life will match theirs.

Most great minds will readily tell you that their vision of greatness was birthed and hatched as they stood on the shoulders of those who had attained greatness before them. Great minds have great habits; one of which is that they carefully select their partners in life. A glimpse into their lives may make a difference in your own life.

WATCH OUT FOR THE NEGATIVE MINDED

Life is too short to associate with negative and shallow minded persons. Be with the people who identify with your values, personality, see your worth and bring out the best in you. According to Henry Ford, "Your best friend is the one who brings out the best in you." So, when you relate with a person or group of persons, always ask yourself whether such relationship is helping you to advance towards your goals in life.

You are responsible for what you have decided to be in life and who you ultimately become. However, you must be very careful in the choices you make with your time and energy and what effort you choose to support. If an organization can also help you to be a better person by discovering the inner you, by giving you challenging opportunities, while you offer your skills, then you are more likely to be in the right place.

Always take time to reevaluate your relationships and their effects. I personally, have in the past been a victim of negative vibrations while volunteering, but refused to allow potentially negative long term effects to take hold. I was doing my graduate program at the New York Law School and I took a volunteer work as Public Relations Officer for the Nigerian Lawyers Association, New York. During the execution of our plan to organize a dinner, I had a conversation with the president and she told me "Shame on you." On another occasion, she negatively told me I was from a different world. On another occasion when we had an event at New York Law School where I assisted in the set-up, after the event, I asked her what advice she would have for me as a young man who wanted to succeed in life and work. Based on her observation and experience, I admitted that I might have made one or two mistakes. She bluntly told me to "go and meet the guys you have been talking to for advice". The humiliation was difficult for me to handle at that time.

During the course of my service, I also had an encounter with the Vice President when I was trying to hone my grammar and writing skills. Instead of being constructive and polite while correcting me with love, she told me, "I have to be hard on you." These words were enough to make me consider resigning from the position because I was only a student at that time and not used to very critical feedback. I wasn't even paid for the job as it was a call to service.

Again, there were many attorneys who refused to step up to handle the challenging position for reasons best known to them. I volunteered because I like leadership opportunities that can help me to grow, but I felt their approach was too harsh.

The moral of this message is that, although this bothered me for a while, I didn't allow this opinion to deflate me totally. Instead, this circumstance fueled me to work harder, to trust myself and prove I could do better. I persevered and even contested for another term which I won unopposed. Three years later, I was called to join the election committee where I participated actively, and to the glory of God, my team and I were able to organize a historic election with the introduction of electronic voting for the association.

Here I am today writing a book about these life challenges and experience. You decide what your life should be despite the challenges that people and situations may bring upon your way. It is up to you not to remain in mediocrity, find the positive lesson in each negative experience, learn by it or let it go.

MAKING A WISE CHOICE OF ASSOCIATION

To figure out whether an individual or organization is a positive or negative time investment in your life, you have to know yourself and what you want in life. It is important to determine your focus, as there are limitless networking opportunities available. Once you get your focus sorted out, you can connect with meetups and organizations that fall into the areas of life that you are passionate about.

If you want to learn about finance, love public speaking or want to be a politician, joining community-based groups is an opportunity you may want to explore. If service to humanity is your passion, then volunteering with clubs like Rotary Club International can place you on the pedestal. These groups can play a big role in bringing out the hidden potentials within you, fine tune your skills and talents, in addition to giving you opportunities which can lead you to the next level in your life.

If all you do with your off time is attend night clubs and social events which have no relevance to your life's progress, then it is a total waste of time. Life is too short to waste it on activities that add no value to your destiny. If an organization can help you to be a better person by helping you discover the inner you and giving you challenging opportunities, then you are most likely in the right place. What is important is how you see yourself in the bigger picture.

Ask yourself, "Where will I be in the next five years if I decide to remain on this path?". If the answer is not pointing in the right direction, then, it's high time you re-evaluate your role in such an association. If need be, disassociate yourself from it and all people who are neither helpful nor relevant to your interests and calling in life. Always take time to reevaluate your relationships and their effects.

I have mentioned it before that your networks often determine your net worth in life. If you have great minds in your network, the ideas and discussions that will flow from your exchanges will trigger a lot of opportunities and information. That may not be the case if you have the wrong people influencing you. In the words of Eleanor Roosevelt, 'Great minds discuss ideas; average minds discuss events; small minds discuss people." It is indeed true that, if you are not informed you are deformed, and once you are deformed, you can't perform because information leads to reformation and transformation.

Networking is one of the key reasons why most people succeed in life. You will never know how far you will go in life if you don't decide to go out of your comfort zone and reach out for greater opportunities. Most people discover themselves through attending events of interest and networking with the right people. That's why it is indispensable to get yourself in the right community and network.

During networking events, you are likely to see successful people sharing their knowledge and success stories among their network, so that others, too, can learn and make progress. That's the beauty of networking.

Note that when you network, it doesn't matter the number of people in the network; all that matters is the productivity of the connection and how it is making you a better person. Moreover, regardless of the size of the network, networking helps you lay a firm foundation for success in life. Without this firm foundation, success may be elusive.

Your network serves as a family and gives you a voice. Families can be small, but they have turned out to be the greatest units that hold a community, nation or country together. Your family gives you an identity. Anybody who wants to know more about you can always look at your family. To apply this here, when you network well, you stand a better chance of being connected to amazing opportunities.

In the labor market, you may have heard of the saying, "It's who you know that gets you the job." However, I believe networking has gone a step higher. The cliché is no longer who you know, but who knows you. This is because you might know the president, CEO,

HR manager or any other influential person in an organization but the question is, do they know you? The point is, someone you know might get you to the door, but someone who knows you will not only open the door for you, but will go ahead to offer you a position.

Now, I must emphasize that networking is not only limited to meeting people and attending events; it has now come to include using social media platforms like Facebook, Instagram, Twitter, Google Plus, Snapchat, and even professional platforms like LinkedIn to connect with people of like passions.

Additionally, research has proven that people who network well easily connect to mentors. Indeed, one of the greatest experiences you may have in life is meeting those people you can consider as mentors; people who can teach and guide you on the principles and secrets of a fulfilled life.

When seeking out a mentor, look for someone who knows how to live by high standards based on your own objectives in life. Your mentors must be people of substance, integrity, and credibility who appreciate your strengths and help you improve on your weaknesses.

You may get virtual mentors that you can emulate, but it is better if you can find real people you can have physical interactions with. This is because of the invaluable experience and exposure that you will get. Their personality, integrity, character, goals, objectives, mission and vision of life must inspire you to reach out of your comfort zone and beyond limited vision or stunted habits.

Please permit me to share the experience of how I met one of my mentors, Dele Momodu. As the Public Relations Officer for the Nigerian Lawyers Association, we were planning to organize an event and I was responsible for researching and recommending a seasoned speaker. I thought he was the most suitable person I could get, but I was in a dilemma as to how to reach him. Still, I tried my luck by reaching out to him on Facebook; and as fate would have it, he responded positively and requested for my phone number. After our engaging conversation, I discovered that we shared a lot in common, and ever since then we have been great friends.

I was able to nurture the friendship and relationship. I was humbled when I reached out to him to write the foreword of this book, and he graciously agreed.

I met two other mentors of mine during an event that I attended in New York City. They are Nkechi Ogbodo, C.E.O., Kechie's Project; and Astrid Sylvester, a life coach. During the meet and greet session, I had an enriching discussion with these two great minds. I told them about my book project and what I intend to achieve with it. Both of them were gracious enough to support me by providing a venue for the book signing and logistics support with their network to get my work out there.

These are great examples of the power of networking.

SERVING IN COMMUNITIES

Every living person is associated with a community. We all need our fellow human beings to survive on earth. According to Mother Teresa, "I can do things you cannot, you can do things I cannot, and together we can do great things."

Serving in communities no doubt has influenced a lot of people in discovering their personality and true worth. For example, your community might want to work on a project and it is in dire need of manpower. Making yourself available in form of volunteering or service can serve as a self-discovery process, apart from the helpful contributions you would be making to your community.

Also, your local church might be in dire need of volunteers to render valuable services during special programs or routine events. Your participation in areas such as the choir, ushering, decorations, protocols, readings, etc., can reveal some unique features about you, as well as opening doors of opportunity for you.

As you must have observed from my second illustration, your community is not limited to your place of birth, where you grew or where you are currently living; it also includes your school, church, and other socio-cultural organizations (corporate or non-governmental organizations) in your neighborhood.

My first call to leadership experience was during my high school days at Federal Government College, Okigwe, in Imo State of Nigeria, where I was responsible for coordinating my fellow students, numbering about 150 during a weekly sanitation exercise. My second real practical experience, where I discovered my leadership capability was during my second year in the university (Madonna University, Nigeria), where I was humbled to have been appointed by the chancellor to be hostel governor and a member of the Students Representative Council. I was literally responsible for about 1,500 students. My duty was primarily to ensure that all the by-laws stipulated by the school authorities were strictly complied with, and and defaulters were reprimanded.

Furthermore, I had the opportunity of serving my community as the youth president of a social-cultural organization called Awareness Movement in the south-eastern part of Nigeria where I came from. The objectives of the association were geared towards enlightening, sensitizing and empowering the youths and the entire community in general about the value of education.

Here's the catch: The experience I got serving my community really influenced me to work on my leadership abilities. I never knew I could achieve so much in life until I served as the president of that noble association. The level of commendation and support I got from my community and my fellow members really humbled me. It made me to believe in my abilities. I must say that the experience proved to be the launch-pad that I needed for greater service to humanity.

The biggest call to service I have ever had was when I emigrated to the United States of America, and joined the Nigerian Lawyers Association, a 501(c)(3) organization based in New York (I said something about this earlier). There I was able to sharpen my leadership experience, as I related with the executive members, association members and the world at large.

Indeed, interacting with members of the community has led to the discovery and development of the potentials of many people. It has given many people the opportunity that they needed to break even. As Henry Ford said, "Coming together is a beginning, staying together is progress, and working together is success."

We all need the society to succeed in life. Without the society and our communities, it will be difficult to be identified in the society. But with your participation in civil activities and communal activities, you learn new things and make new discoveries.

BOTTOM-LINE

We need our fellow human beings to survive. Reaching out to the world includes the association we belong to, the kind of networking events we identify with, as well as the roles we play when serving in our communities, associations, churches, other social gatherings. Your roles in these associations and organizations really help to define your personality and, to a reasonable extent, they can help to determine where you will be in the near future, all things being equal.

FOOD FOR THOUGHT

If you have the right information, men of honor will respect you. If you have wisdom, you will be revered. The more you network right, the more opportunities, knowledge and information you gain in life.

In politics, for you to be respected, revered and desired, you must have either economic or political power, in addition to having grassroots support. But should you have both powers, you will be highly sought after because you will be considered a potential game-changer.

Serving and networking in the community have greatly influenced and empowered a lot of people to discover themselves. Engaging in meaningful service and networking will take you farther and higher in life than you could ever imagine. I strongly encourage you to always make yourself available whenever and wherever you find opportunities to serve. You never can tell what discovery or contribution you will make.

Some individuals discovered their acting or singing prowess by performing in churches and schools; and with the right support and motivation, they went on to become great achievers, role models and celebrities. You are the next in line!

ACTION EXERCISE

1. Do you belong to any association(s)? What influences have they had on your life?

2. What is the mission/vision of your association (or organization)?

3. Do you believe in the objectives of the association?

4. Do you like to network? Has it in any way influenced you? If yes, where and how has this happened? Finally, would you recommend it to your friends?

LAST NOTES

The end is just the beginning. Just when you think you already know all about yourself, you discover that there is always room for growth where a new experience or situation demands it. You may or may not meet the goal but your worthy effort will certainly be noticed.

Always allow learning and growth to permeate your life. This way, you continue to improve yourself while rendering great service. In your own unique way, you would have designed your own destiny and come to live a full life of success.

In summary, let me state that, while you have a lot to do in deciding your destiny, God is the ultimate designer of our destiny. Yes, we are also partakers in the designing of our destiny. This is because we contribute in shaping our destiny in one way or the other due to the choices and decisions we make. Still, the Creator, Master and Ruler of the universe, mankind and destinies is God Almighty. It is, therefore, in our interest that we acknowledge Him in all we do and let Him have the final say in our lives!

Finally, before you close this book. I have two questions for you.

1. Name three things that you appreciate about this book and how it has helped you to design your destiny?

2. Will you recommend it to your friends?

Made in the USA
Middletown, DE
23 December 2022

20212430R00086